Alev Masarwa

Memory, Mimesis, and the Modern

WWU
MÜNSTER

Wissenschaftliche Schriften der WWU Münster

Reihe XII

Band 34

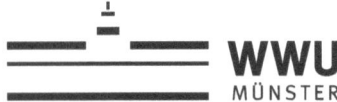

Alev Masarwa

Memory, Mimesis, and the Modern

The Literary Heritage in Māmayh's Poetry

Georg Olms Verlag
Hildesheim · Zürich · New York

Wissenschaftliche Schriften der WWU Münster
herausgegeben von der Universitäts- und Landesbibliothek Münster
http://www.ulb.uni-muenster.de

Eine Publikation in Zusammenarbeit mit dem Georg Olms Verlag
https://www.olms.de

OLMS

Bibliografische Information der Deutschen Nationalbibliothek:
Die Deutsche Nationalbibliothek verzeichnet diese Publikation in der Deutschen Nationalbibliografie; detaillierte bibliografische Daten sind im Internet über https://www.dnb.de abrufbar.

Dieses Buch steht gleichzeitig in einer elektronischen Version über den Publikations- und Archivierungsserver der WWU Münster zur Verfügung.
https://www.ulb.uni-muenster.de/wissenschaftliche-schriften

Alev Masarwa
„Memory, Mimesis, and the Modern. The Literary Heritage in Māmayh's Poetry"
Wissenschaftliche Schriften der WWU Münster, Reihe XII, Band 34
Georg Olms Verlag, Hildesheim

ISBN	978-3-487-16216-4	(Druckausgabe Georg Olms Verlag)
ISBN	978-3-8405-0274-3	(elektronische Version)
DOI	10.17879/33069637534	(elektronische Version)
URN	urn:nbn:de:hbz:6-33069638049	(elektronische Version)

direkt zur Online-Version:

Satz: Alev Masarwa
Umschlag: ULB Münster

Contents

Memory, mimesis, and the modern: The literary heritage in Māmayh's poetry 3
Memoria: timeline of transience 13
Mimesis: imitatio-aemulatio as poetic memory 21
Taḫmīs-poems: amplifying the paragons 22
Taḍmīn: a stylistic variation on a theme 31
The modern 47
Constrained writing 48
Coffee poems 51
Appendix 65
Bibliography 73

Memory, Mimesis, and the Modern: the Literary Heritage in Māmayh's Poetry

Māmayh Muḥammad b. Aḥmad b. ʿAbdallāh ar-Rūmī ad-Dimašqī (d. ca. 986 or 987/1578–9) was one of the most significant Damascan poets of the 10th/16th century.[1] His verses were sung from Damascus to Yemen, and his epigrammatic chronograms decorate many buildings founded by Ottoman governors. Little is known about his scholarly education and poetic training. However, Māmayh's poems and particularly their addressees indicate that he was a major figure in the intellectual life of Damascus, participating in its vivid and contentious literary gatherings (*maǧālis*) and keeping close ties to the administrative elites of Damascus and the chief *muftī* in Istanbul Abū s-Suʿūd Efendī (Turkish: Ebüssuûd Efendi, d.

---

1 On his life and poetic work see also Šaraf ad-Dīn Ibn Ayyūb: *Kitab ar-rawḍ al-ʿāṭir*, ed. Mašhūr al-Ḥabbāzī, 2 vols. (Beirut: Dār al-Kutub al-ʿIlmiyyah, 1441/2020), 2:944–59. For alternative vocalizations and transcriptions of his name (Māmayh, Māmāy, Māmiyyah, Māmayyah, and Māmiyh corresponding to Mami resp. Memi, the Turkish short form for Muḥammad resp. Mehmet) see Alev Masarwa: "Māmayh Muḥammad b. Aḥmad b. ʿAbdallāh ar-Rūmī", in: *Encyclopaedia of Islam Three* (upcoming). On his life and poetic work see Brockelmann: *GAL* 2:271–2 and *GALS* 2:382; Šihāb ad-Dīn al-Ḫafāǧī: *Ḫabāyā z-zawāyā fī mā fī r-riǧāl min al-baqāyā*, eds. Muḥammad Masʿūd Arkīn [Ergin] et al. (Damascus, Maṭbūʿāt Maǧmaʿ al-Luġah al-ʿArabiyyah bi-Dimašq, 1436/2010), 192–97; al-ʿAydarūs: *An-Nūr as-sāfir ʿan aḫbār al-qarn al-ʿāšir*, eds. Aḥmad Ḥālū et al. (Beirut: Dār Ṣādir, 2001), 396–402 and 466–7; Clifford Edmund Bosworth: "A Janissary poet of sixteenth-century Damascus", in: *Essays in honor of Bernard Lewis. The Islamic world, classical and medieval, Ottoman and modern*, eds C. E. Bosworth et al. (Princeton: Darwin Press, 1989), 451–66; Masarwa: "Performing the Occasion: The Chronograms of Māmayya ar-Rūmī", in: *The Mamluk-Ottoman Transition: Continuity and Change in Egypt and Bilād al-Shām in the Sixteenth Century*, eds. Stephan Conermann et al. (Göttingen: Vandenhoeck & Ruprecht Verlage, 2017), 177–206.

982/1574).[2] There are over twenty copies of Māmayh's voluminous *dīwān Rawḍat al-muštāq wa-bahǧat al-ʿuššāq* (Garden of the ardent yearner and the joy of the lovers) in existence, which consists of over 1,300 poems. The *dīwān* demonstrates Māmayh's excellent command of most of the classical poetic genres and his enthusiasm for more modern forms of poetry. Apart from eulogies to the prophet and the Ottoman sultans, as well as city panegyrics, Māmayh elaborates on topics like coffee, love, drugs, and music. Though fluent in Ottoman, he almost exclusively – except in his bilingual *mulammaʿ*-poems – wrote in Arabic, as he felt at home in Damascus.[3]

Based on the current results of the ongoing edition of Māmayh's *dīwān*, this study discusses a selection of poems in which the poet engages with the literary past by using mimetic and emulative techniques (like *taḍmīn*, *iqtibās*, and *taḫmīs* poems) but also those in which Māmayh exhibits more modern stylistic modes, forms and topics (like *ʿāṭil* verses, coffee poems, and vernacular poems).[4] While the mimetic poems refer directly to the admired or canonized models of the past perpetuating the tradition into

---

2 Ibn Ayyūb: *Kitab ar-rawḍ al-ʿāṭir*, 2:925–30.

3 Māmayh used different pen names (*maḫlas*). While he bragged about his Rūmī descendance, he also boasted of his homeland Syria, declaiming, esp. in his *zaǧals*: (*a*)*nā* [...] *qayyim aš-Šām* (I am ... the master/bard of Syria).

4 'Modern' is not necessarily the counterpart of 'classical', it is – within the system of pre-modern poetry – the continuation of it in the form of actualization (see below). As will also be emphasized, the poetic forms presented in the section 'modern' are not new at all. 'Modern' initially serves as a surrogate for the 'new' to avoid the fetishism attached to it until an adequate basis ('medium' in the following) which justifies its use is established. One could use the word 'new', as long as it does not designate the 'new' as an absolute term but as a relative one. In some cases, the term is synonymous to 'unconventional', 'playful', 'not worn-out', in others to 'contemporary', 'en vogue', or 'the literary modern'.

the poet's present, the focus of the contemporary topics in the *dīwān* is on how the poet's present was connected to the poetic and aesthetic practices of the past. By analyzing selected poems, this study offers evidence of the impressive literary and intellectual background of an initially Ottomanized and then 'Syrianized' (former soldier-) poet, as well as showing his tremendous poetic creativity in melding together the 'old' and the 'new' in his verse.

The general verdict of a decline in literature,[5] and thus of Islamic culture over several epochs, not only ignores the mass of literary testimonies but has also led to a complete shift in responsibility (to provide evidence) to the side of the literary creators. Except for some generalizing, albeit serious judgments such as "absence of creativity and loss of vigor"[6], the paradigm of decline is "an unexamined opinion imposed on us without proof"[7]. Subsequently, since only a comparatively small number of works from this 'period of decline' have been studied, there is still a lot of basic

5 See Dana Sajdi: "Decline, Its Discontents and Ottoman Cultural History: By Way of Introduction", in: *Ottoman Tulips, Ottoman Coffee: Leisure and Lifestyle in the Eighteenth Century*, eadem (London and New York: I.B. Tauris, 2014), 1–40 for an overview of the decline-thesis and the scholarly efforts to dismantle the category of decline, and Manfred Sing: "The Decline of Islam and the Rise of Inḥiṭāṭ: The Discrete Charm of Language Games about Decadence in the 19th and 20th Centuries", in: *Inḥiṭāṭ – The Decline Paradigm: Its Influence and Persistence in the Writing of Arab Cultural History*, ed. Syrinx von Hees (Würzburg: Ergon-Verlag, 2017), 1–70.

6 Joseph E. Lowry and Devin J. Stewart: "Introduction", in: *Essays in Arabic Literary Biography 1350–1850*, ed. by Joseph E. Lowry and Devin J. Stewart (Wiesbaden: Harrassowitz, 2009), 1–12, here 1.

7 Michael Beard in his review of "Essays in Arabic Literary Biography 1350–1850", in: *Journal of the American Oriental Society* 132 (2012), 486–488, here 486.

research to be done in many respects.[8] Literary criticism has mostly avoided engagement with the literary past or even added to the paradigm of decline and thus has aided the all too superficial fetish for 'the new' in modernity. Therefore, to defy this imbalance, the use of the word is avoided in the rest of what follows as much as possible, as the uninhibited chasing of the 'new' is only a correlate for the concept of decline on the positive axis.

Māmayh's *dīwān*, besides classical poetry, is full of literary forms that are unconventional – be they 'minor' or 'inferior' literary forms. They need not be 'new' per se just to be considered of literary merit. Such an understanding ignores pre-modern literary traditions, which unfold their innovative and form-creating capacities not only through the momentum of *inventio*, but far more from the various techniques of *tractatio materiae*, among them the techniques of *memoria*, *imitatio* and *aemulatio*. Since in most cases we cannot determine the author or the exact time of creation of every 'new' literary form, caution is required when labelling something as such. New things usually arise unnoticed, as Shklovsky (1893–1984) points out: "New phenomena accumulate without being perceived, later they are perceived in a revolutionary way."[9] In literature, this also applies to discovering the new in retrospect, since the 'new' needs a discourse or a medium in order to be grasped,[10] but also a precise

8 However, for the period in question, *Essays in Arabic Literary Biography 1350–1850* can be considered a pioneering work for the reassessment of the literary history. See also bibliographical references in Fn. 11 and Fn. 13.

9 Viktor B. Shklovsky in Annie van den Oever: "'Ostranenie', 'The Montage of Attractions' and Early Cinema's 'Properly Irreducible Alien Quality'", in: *Ostrannenie. On "Strangeness" and the Moving Image. The History, Reception, and Relevance of a Conceptnull*, ed. eadem (Amsterdam: Amsterdam University Press, 2010), 56.

10 Tom Gunning: "Re-Newing Old Technologies: Astonishment, Second Nature, and the Un-canny in Technology from the Previous Turn-of-the-Century", in:

knowledge of what preceded it. However, such a discursive platform (or a medium) does not emerge by itself. The literary history of the 16th century can only be properly grasped if its source texts are read closely and if it is embedded in the larger context of the preceding and subsequent centuries.[11]

Regarding Māmayh's poetry as a particular case, it is therefore of interest to find out how much a janissary who had moved to Damascus could learn from the heritage of Arabic literature in order to be able to assert himself as a poet in the face of this extremely powerful tradition. Furthermore, looking at Māmayh's prospective reception, this approach enhances a better understanding of his impact on subsequent generations and how his poems have been handed down to those generations. The large number of surviving manuscripts of Māmayh's *dīwān*, their design variants, the various notes, etc., already indicate the form and frequency in which this memory work on Māmayh was carried out.

This is not the place to analyse every aspect of the impact of the Arabic literary legacy on Māmayh's compositions and vice versa, so I will only

Rethinking Media Change: The Aesthetics of Transition, eds. David Thorburn et al. (Cambridge [Mass.]: MIT Press, 2003), 39, 44 n. 20.

11 Over the last few decades, an increasing number of promising studies on Arabic literature in the Ottoman era have been published. See also Fn. 5 and 6. Among those, dealing more specifically with Syrian poets are: Usāmah ʿAnūtī: *al-Ḥarakah al-adabiyyah fī bilād aš-Šām ḫilāl al-qarn aṯ-ṯamin ʿašar* (Beirut: Lebanese University Press, 1970), based on a massive amount of manuscripts. Further the studies of Zaynab Bīrahğaklī: esp. her *al-Ḥarakah aš-šiʿriyyah fī Ḥalab: fī l-qarn al-ḥādī ʿašar al-hiğrī* (ʿAmmān: Dār aḍ-Ḍiyāʾ, 1444/2001) and more recently İbrahim Fidan: *Osmanlı Dönemi Arap Şairlerinden İbnu'n Nakib el-Huseyni* (Ankara: Gece Kitaplığı, 2016), Mücahit Küçüksarı: *Osmanlı Dönemi Arap Şairlerinden İbrahim Es-Sefercelani ve Şiirleri* (Konya: Çizgi Kitabevi, 2017), and Yusuf Sami Samancı: *Osmanlı dönemi Arap Şairlerinden Mencek Paşa ve Şiirleri* (Konya: Çizgi Kitabevi, 2017).

touch on those poems that are directly relevant to the topic of this study and will therefore use the themes of 'memory' and 'mimesis' (imitatio/ aemulatio) to deal with some aspects of Māmayh's poetry that show tangible traces of the literary heritage and the artfulness with which the literary past was actualized into the poet's present. Regarding the 'modern' I will discuss the poems that exhibit more novel styles, forms, and themes and show how, in turn, they are connected to the conventions of the poetic art of the past. In this context, 'modern' is not used to point to a designated epoch, nor as a qualifying contrast, superior to conventional poetry.[12] Instead, it non-judgementally conveys the range of 'new arts' (*al-funūn al-mustaḥdaṯah*)[13] of pre-modern poetry that share also formal similarities with what encompasses the *poesis artificiosa*,[14] which had its heyday in the baroque literature.

The range of poetic arts displayed in Māmayh's *Dīwān* goes beyond what even later poetological manuals have subsumed under *al-funūn as-sabʿa*

12 See Fn. 4.

13 Among the most comprehensive studies for the 'new arts' are Bakrī Šayḫ Amīn: *Muṭālaʿāt fī š-šiʿr al-Mamlūkī wa-l-ʿUṯmānī* (Cairo: Dār aš-Šurūq, 1972); Muḥammad Altunǧī (not al-Tunǧī): *al-Ittiǧāhāt aš-šiʿriyyah fī bilād aš-Šām fī l-ʿaṣr al-ʿUṯmānī: dirāsah* (Damascus: Ittiḥād al-Kuttāb al-ʿArab, 1993) and the unpublished dissertation of ʿId Fatḥī ʿAbd al-ʿAzīz: *al-Ittiǧahāt al-adab al-ʿarabī fī l-qarn al-ḥādī ʿašar al-hiǧrī* (Diss., ʿAyn Šams University: Kulliyat al-Ādāb, Cairo 1426–27/2005–6).

14 The term refers to elaborate poetic forms, meters, and to extraordinary practices in use of word order and puns. The poetic practice of *poesis artificiosa* had already been acknowledged in the literary heritage of both the ancient Greeks and Romans and in the Far and Middle East. See the introductory remarks by Agnieszka Borysowska and Barbara Milewska-Waźbińska: "Introductionary Note", in: *Poesis Artificiosa. Between Theory and Practice*, ed. eadem (Frankfurt, a. M.: Peter Lang Acad. Research, 2013), 7.

(seven arts)[15] and *al-funūn al-mustaḥdaṯah* (new arts). Applied to poetry, the 'new arts' denote an ever-varied set of poetic forms, meters, and techniques, distinct from the more conventional *qaṣīdah*, its *aġrād* and diction (*fuṣḥā* and (semi-)vernacular). Though their number changes, the so called 'seven arts' (*al-funūn as-sab'a*) – included in the 'new arts' – are an earlier established term for the newer prosodic genres (traditionally *muwaššah, zağal, mawālīyā, dūbayt, kān wa-kān, and qūmā*, additionally also *ḥammāq, bullayqah* and *silsilah*) some of which are written in *fuṣḥā* and others in the (semi-) vernacular.

15 See e.g., Hakan Özkan: *Geschichte des östlichen zağal – dialektale arabische Strophendichtung aus dem Osten der arabischen Welt von ihren Anfängen bis zum Ende der Mamlukenzeit* (Baden-Baden: Ergon-Verlag, 2020).

Memoria

Memoria: Timeline of Transience

Of the five phases that mark the development of persuasive speech, *memoria* (Greek: mneme) is the fourth element in the canon of classical rhetoric.[16] Here, however, *memoria* will be examined less as a component of the art of speech composition of Greco-Roman rhetoric than as an act of remembering and as a literary technique.[17] There are, of course, many points of reference in Māmayh's poetry that can exemplify this, but in the following poem these two aspects are particularly evident. The poem [#228][18] consists of 40 verses (41 in some mss.) – a number which as will be shown is symbolically significant – and is one of Māmayh's later compositions, written sometime after the death of Selīm II. (d. 1574). The poem – composed in the form of an admonition – combines the invocation of the act of remembering, i.e., derived from the repository of historical memory along with its counterpart, forgetting. Māmayh opens with an impressive warning, immediately introducing the theme sustained

---

16 The five production stages of a speech are *inventio, dispositio, elocutio, memoria,* and *pronuntiatio*. For *memoria* within the *opera oratoris* see Terry V.F. Brogan: "Rhetoric and Poetry", in: *The New Princeton Encyclopedia of Poetry and Poetics,* eds. Alex Preminger, Terry V.F. Brogan et al. (Princeton, N.J.: Princeton University Press, 1993), 1048 and Rüdiger Zymner: "Rhetorik, Literatur und Literaturwissenschaft", in: *Handbuch Literarische Rhetorik*, ed. Rüdiger Zymner (Berlin/Boston: de Gruyter, 2015), 8.

17 For the conceptional history of *memoria* as a personal/episodic, semantic/historical, collective-cultural, and literary memorial repository (Erinnerungsspeicher) see Wolfgang Neuber: "memoria", in: *Reallexikon der deutschen Literaturwissenschaft*, eds. Georg Braungart et al. (Berlin/New York: de Gruyter, 2007), 562–66. For the arts of memory as a *techne* see Renate Lachmann: "Cultural Memory and the Role of Literature", in: *European Review* 12 (2004), 165–78.

18 The numbering of the poems is based on MS. Wetzstein II 243, Staatsbibliothek zu Berlin. The corresponding folio numbers are provided in the appendix. (?) A question mark indicates poems that are unclear either in their spelling or in terms of their use of figurative language in the manuscripts.

throughout the poem of a warning against the illusion of permanence in a transient world:

[#228] وقال يذكر القرونَ الماضيةَ [من الرمل]

1 لَيْسَ لِلنَّاسِ مِنَ المَوْتِ مَفَرْ   وَلَكَمْ غَيَّبَ بَدْواً وَحَضَرْ

2 وَإِذَا فَكَّرَ فِيهِ عَاقِلٌ   سَكَبَ العَبْرَةَ مِنْ هَوْلِ الْعِبَرْ

3 كَيْفَ فِي دَارِ الفَنَا يُرْجَى الْبَقَا   إِنَّ هَذَا مِنْ خَيَالَاتِ الْفِكَرْ

4 فَازَ مَنْ قَدَّمَ أُخْرَاهُ عَلَى   هَذِهِ الدُّنْيَا وَبِالْمَوْتِ اعْتَبَرْ

5 أَيْنَ يَا مَغْرُورُ قُلْ لِي آدَمُ   أَيْنَ إِدْرِيسُ وَنُوحٌ فِي الْبَشَرْ

6 أَيْنَ أَهْلُ الرَّسِّ وَالإِبْلِ الَّذِي   عَبَدُوا مِنْ جَهْلِهِمْ حَتَّى الشَّجَرْ

7 أَيْنَ إِبْرَاهِيمُ أَعْنِي بِالَّذِي   قَدْ بَنَى البَيْتَ المُعَلَّى وَالْحَجَرْ

1 From death there is no escape for people / and how many has it taken away, be they dwellers of towns or desert?

2 And when a sane mind thinks about it, / he will only shed tears for all the warning lessons.

3 How can one long for dwelling in a house which is transient / for this (wish to stay) is only an illusion?

4 Only he is safe who gives the hereafter a precedence / over the worldly life and draws lessons from (inevitable) death.

5 Tell me, haughty fellow, where are Adam, Idrīs and Noah amongst us now?

6 Where are the people of ar-Rass and the people of the camel / who out of their ignorance even worshipped trees?[19]

7 And where is Abraham, I mean the one who erected the Sublime Abode (Kaʿbah) and (placed therein the Black) Stone?[20]

With aphoristic and sententious moralizing, the poet draws an episodic timeline of transience (*vanitas*) from Adam to Selim II by giving examples of prophets, people, and nations of the Quran and then historical persons, caliphs, dynasties etc., which had all perished by the lifetime of the poet. Nevertheless, and regardless of these famous names in charge of history, death is seen to advance. The poet cannot offer a real counter concept, as death is inevitable, and strikes all people, dynasties and of course him. Usually, in such sententious poetry one would expect the emphasis to be on a note of high moral value, as best exemplified or impersonated by an exemplary person/figure, who represented an ideal that mankind failed to adhere to for some reason. But even those figures have vanished. Therefore, the moral message persists in the act of reminding as an antidote to cultural amnesia, and the poet seeks protection and shelter in God for himself and the reader[21] while leaving his poem behind as a beautiful reminder. Māmayh used this same pattern of re-enacting *memoria* within another poem (*zağal* #1149) using similar phrasing:

19 See "people of Rass" in Q 25:38 and 50:12 as people/companions of the camel, see also Q 38:13 for the *aṣḥāb al-aykah* (dwellers of the wood).

20 The complete poem and its translation are provided in the appendix. Unless otherwise noted, all translations are my own.

21 Here, the prophet is not involved as an intercessor as is usual in panegyrical odes with a similar content.

[#1149] (زجل)

أَيْنَ هُود وَأَيْنَ عَادْ ° وَأَيْنَ شَدَّادْ   وَأَيْنَ ذِي الأَوْتَادْ ° وَأَيْنَ إِسْكَنْدَرْ

وَأَيْنَ سُلَيْمَانْ ° وَحُكْمُهْ فِي الجَانْ   أَيْنَ كِسْرَى نُعْمَانْ ° أَيْنَ ملك قَيْصَرْ

أَيْنَ صَرْحُ هَامَانْ ° أَيْنَ ملك سَاسَانْ   أَيْنَ الَّذِي كَانَ ° لَهُ صِيتٌ فِي حِمْيَرْ

Where is Hūd, and where is ʿĀd and where is Šaddād? / And where is Pharaoh (lit.: owner of the stakes), and where is Iskandar?

And where is Sulaymān with his command over the *ǧinn*? / And where is king Nuʿmān and where is the kingdom of (or read *malik*: king) Caesar?

And where is the edifice of Hāmān and where is the power of Sāsān? / And where is the one, who had honor among the Ḥimyar?[22]

The admonition in #228 is realized by a) listing those gone and forgotten, and b) by the unabated repetition (*tikrār*) of the phrase (*ayna xy* and *ayna man*) which invokes remembrance either through nostalgic portrayals (similar to *aṭlāl* motives) or with negative examples from the past:

---

22 Also, Ibn Dāniyāl's (d. 710/1310) hero Ġarīb remembers his better days in a similar way, see Georg Jacob: *Ein ägyptischer Jahrmarkt im 13. Jahrhundert* (München: Verlag der Königlich Bayerischen Akademie der Wissenschaften, 1910), 6.

Performing memoria

(x) + fabula +

what x is associated with (+ *iqtibās*, …)

(y) + fabula +

what y is associated with (+ *iqtibās*, ...)

} + *ayna* → enacts memoria → admonition

The poet presents the past chronologically from the repository of historical memory but calls the names into the present by telling associated fabula, amplified with allusions (*talmīḥ*) or quotations (*iqtibās*) from the Quran (as a memorial text/*Gedächtnistext*). The first device lists case studies (x, y, z) chronologically, emphasizing the aspect of variation, and the second, the repetition (*tikrār*), de-historicizes them at the same time. Such techniques operate with central aspects of memoria oscillating between passive aggregates and active apparatuses that generate actualizations from recollections and transformations of the older patterns.[23] When we ignore the *ayna*-phrase, this poetic form resembles the versified ruler lists for certain regions and dynasties, known since Mamluk times.

In a different context, I have referred to the pattern of memory and the legitimized Ottoman rule in poem #228.[24] Of further interest, however, is who is enlisted and who is left out. Who occupies more space within the verses and who less, and how are they remembered? As many of the persons mentioned here are also patron saints of specific professions, is there

---

23 Frauke Berndt: "Poetische Topik", in: *Handbuch Literarische Rhetorik*, ed. Rüdiger Zymner (Berlin/Boston: de Gruyter, 2015), 440.

24 Masarwa, "Performing the Occasion: The Chronograms of Māmayya ar-Rūmī", in: *The Mamluk-Ottoman Transition: Continuity and Change in Egypt and Bilād al-Shām in the Sixteenth Century*, eds. Stephan Conermann et al. (Göttingen: Vandenhoeck & Ruprecht Verlage, 2017), 197–98.

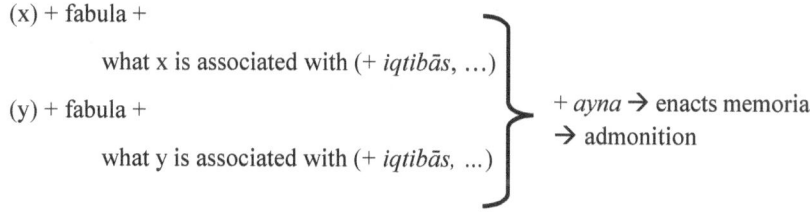

perhaps an allusion to them? Only Moses (v. 12–v. 13) and Muḥammad (v. 23–v. 24) are given two full lines. Between Jesus and the Prophet Muḥammad the Greeks, the Persians and Romans are impersonated metonymically (synecdoche) by Plato and Aristoteles, Banū Sāsān and Khusraw and Caesar. Of course, it is no coincidence that the prophet Muḥammad, though given a central place around the middle of the poem, does not re-occur at its end. This might be considered contrary to the conventions for the final section of such panegyrics, but it strictly follows the logic of the poetic idea.

Mimesis

Mimesis: Imitatio-Aemulatio as Poetic Memory

Regarding the devices of mimesis and its special significance for the aesthetic production in Arabic poetry, here, too, we are less interested in those aspects that have to do with *The Representation of Reality in Literature*. Moreover, we will concentrate on those that operate on the general level artfully with intertextuality as the "memory of literature."[25] The focus is thus on poems that contain a recognizable trace or a clear image of literary predecessors and employ a deliberate technique of appropriation and emulation with different modes of engagement.

For memoria we have focused on remembrance as a literary topic and device, whereas with mimesis in our context we refer to all those techniques of writing in response to authorial and textual models, i.e., those that are in a diachronic dialogue with tradition. Among these are numerous poetic forms such as *iqtibās* epigrams, *taḍmīn* verses, *muʿāraḍah* poems, and from the musical field the contrafactual compositions created according to certain song and melody patterns (*maqām*, modes), which all appear in Māmayh's *dīwān*.[26] Here, I will focus on *taẖmīs* poems and *taḍmīn* epigrams, because they clearly illustrate different imitation techniques in those poems where the original text is co-present. They demonstrate what Māmayh not only acquired from literary tradition but mastered to such an extent that he was able to integrate or modify it in his own poetry.

---

25 Lachmann: "Mnemonic and Intertextual Aspects of Literature", 301–10.

26 For details of the literary techniques of *iqtibās* and *taḍmīn* in Māmayh's epigrams see Masarwa: "Poetisch wider Willen: Der Koran im Vers Māmayhs. Über poetische Verfahren der Doppel- bzw. Mehrfachcodierung und des Code-Switching in *iqtibās*-Epigrammen", in: *Doing Justice to a Wronged Literature: Essays in Honour of Professor Thomas Bauer on his Sixtieth Birthday*, eds. Hakan Özkan and Nefeli Papoutsakis (Leiden: Brill, upcoming 2022).

Since the so-called "genius period," the negative attitude towards mimetic and emulative artworks as a less valuable form of art has been prevalent in literary criticism.[27] However, the dismissive conclusion that imitation is merely a recycling of literary heritage is not sufficient to understand the creative energies applied to a paragon text.

Taḫmīs-Poems: Amplifying the Paragons

The *taḫmīs* (pl. *taḫāmīs*, *taḫmisāt*, literally: turning into/to make five) is a literary device of amplification of an already existing poem and simultaneously one of the various forms of *taḍmīn*. The poet adds three hemistichs of his own to the first hemistich (*ṣadr*-verse) of a poem (base poem or source poem), resulting in five hemistichs with the original distichon. The meter of the base poem is usually not changed, but in rhyme the new hemistichs are aligned with the *ṣadr* verse (hereafter I-a or *ṣadr al-aṣl*) of the base poem. Thus, the actual rhyming letter is flanked by four rhyming words, which can always change depending on the original half-verse (I-a), which in itself is not a rhyme carrier. Formally, the *ʿağuz*-verse of the base poem (I-b) with the weighty rhyme accent is counterbalanced by four hemistichs, as in the following scheme:

.a ----ـهـ

.b ----ـهـ

.c ----ـهـ

.1 ----ـهـ ----م

I-a (صدر الأصل) I-b (عجز الاصل)

27 For a discussion of such a valuation of *taḫmīses*, see Masarwa: "Māmayh im Prophetenmantel: Ornat, Saum und Zipfel der *Burdah* im *Taḫmīs*", in: *Emerging Forms of Piety Centering on Muḥammad as Reflected in Arabic Literature*, ed. Ines Weinrich (Baden-Baden: Ergon, upcoming 2022).

Commonly, base texts were those which, like the *Burdah*, were on everyone's lips, or particularly artful poems on which the poets could display their own skills in adding variations. This was thus work based on the classics with which a poetic dialogue from text to text (or poet to poet) and, likewise, a dialogue with the poetic tradition was created. The challenge for a *taḫmīs* writer is not only in the prosodic realm but also in the content. The poet cannot give free rein to his creative power, since the amplifications remain within the semantics of the original verse and work toward realization in the *ʿağuz*-verse (I-b) of the base poem. Selected *qaṣīdahs* may themselves contain *taḍmīn* verses, or Quranic verses (*iqtibās*), and they may also be, in themselves, a *muʿāraḍah* to another poem. All these different levels and varieties in the base poem must be considered by the younger poet in his expansion, since he does not change the theme or the rhyme. The high rank of the original poem is also not questioned in principle in the *taḫmīsāt* and, unlike in a *muʿāraḍah*, for example, is explicitly maintained. Amplifying entire poems, especially longer ones, was, moreover, still an active demonstration of appreciation of the original poem and its author through participation (ex-post co-writing) in the given pattern. Nevertheless, there are structural mechanisms for varying the hierarchy and framework of the original poem or for directing the reader's attention to the amplified verses. This is accomplished, for example, in purely formal terms in the various presentation techniques of the *taḫmīses* on the page, depending on where the author, in our cases mostly the copyist or his scribal convention, wants to direct the reader's attention: to the amplified verses, or the *ʿağuz*-verse with the concise rhyme, or to the verses of the original poem (I-a and I-b), which together take on a strophic form (see images of presentation techniques of *taḫmīses*).

Furthermore, there are compositional procedures employed by the *taḫmīs* author himself, e.g., by a) amplifying only a certain number of verses from the original poem and thus adjusting the plot and thematic weighting of the base poem, or b) placing them in a different order and consequently interfering with the plot. Amplifying a selection has similar stylistic backgrounds to *taḍmīn* practices: the poet could emphasize certain stylistic figures, add them, shift the original compositional framework, and thereby give the unchanged *ʿağuz*-verse a different realization while expanding the dimensions of its meaning.

The source poems used were sometimes those that only entered the stage of aesthetic discourse through their amplification or those that were extremely famous. Particularly frequent with Māmayh are *ghazal*-poems and sufic religious poems, many Andalusian poems, and predominantly those which originate from the 11th to 13th centuries. Among the few contemporary authors is Abū s-Suʿūd, whose *Mīmiyyah* (itself a *muʿāraḍah* to Ibn ʿArabī) Māmayh has amplified completely. But in general, choosing a poem from a contemporary poet and at best from one's own intellectual circle increased the poet's reputation and was a means of literary communication.

Māmayh provides an exceptional *taḫmīs* in two respects, firstly because he wrote a *taḫmīs* on his own poem (#839 with 24 verses) and secondly because it is a scathing poem about a contemporary from Nāblus, (*al-Fātūšī l-kaḏḏāb*) al-Fātūšī the Liar. The amplification increases the poem from 24 to 60 distichs and thus increases expressions in coarse language with a tremendous effect: it breaks his opponent into pieces! A further exceptional *taḫmīs* is one Māmayh wrote on the Mantle poem by al-Būṣīrī which he called *Quṭb al-arbaʿīn wa-llāhu al-muʿīn* (Pole of the forties and God is the [real] protector).[28] Amplifying the *Burdah* was almost a pious activity and Māmayh of course did it for the entire poem (160–163 verses yielding 400 distichs; in most mss. in 640–652 lines), claiming that his *taḫmīs* was the 41st of all the *taḫmīsāt* – a number that is significant because Māmayh alludes to the genre of 40-*ḥadīṯ* (*al-arbaʿūn*)collections and 40 previously written *taḫmīsāt*, at the top of which is his 41st *taḫmīs*.

28 *Muʿīn* can also be read as *maʿīn*, i.e., the spring/origin.

Less famous but also admired by Māmayh and his contemporaries was the Syrian poet Ibn Mulayk al-Ḥamawī.[29] The *ghazal* (#347) is originally an eight-liner, of which Māmayh skips the fourth verse and amplifies seven, but in addition – as is often the case in the *taḫmīsāt* in the *dīwān* – changes the original order of the verses (I-V-II-III-VI-VII-VIII).

Taḫmīs #347: Māmayh with Ibn Mulayk al-Ḥamawī

وله تخميسٌ [أبيات بن مُليك الحموي]　　　　[بحر المنسرح]

\129ب\ حَيًّا فَأَحْيَا الْوَرَى مُحَيَّاهُ

وَالثَّغْرُ أَنشى الطِّلا حُمَيَّاه

وَرِيقُهُ الْعَذْبُ فِي ثَنَايَاهُ

نَمَّ عَلَى الْمِسْكِ طِيبُ رَيَّاهُ　　　　غَزَالُ سِرْبٍ تَبَارَكَ اللهُ [1]

يَا لَايِمِي كُفَّ عَنْ مَلَامِي [و] إِنْ

سَأَلتَ عَمَّنْ بِهِ الْفُؤَادُ فُتِنْ

وَفِي صَمِيمِ الْحَشَا هَوَاهُ كُمِنْ

غَزَالُ سِرْبٍ مِنَ الْعُيُونِ وَمِنْ　　　　حُشَاشَتِي مَاؤُهُ وَمَرْعَاهُ [5]

لِلّهِ فِي هَجْرِهِ الشَّجِي وَلَهُ

29　Ibn Ayyūb: *Kitab ar-rawḍ al-ʿāṭir*, 2:905. See also Masarwa: "Ibn Mulayk", in: *Encyclopaedia of Islam Three* (2022).

كَمْ زَادَ فِي مُهْجَتِي لَهُ وَلَهُ

كَمْ قَايِلٍ وَالدَّلَالُ مَيَّلَهُ

قَوَامُهُ ذُو الجَلَالِ عدَّله   وَصَاغَهُ فِتْنَةً وَسَوَّاهُ [2]

جَلَّ الَّذِي فِي الْمِلَاحِ جَمَّلَهُ

وَفِتْنَةً لِلأَنَامِ أَرْسَلَهُ

وَالْوَجْهُ بَدْرُ السَّمَاءِ كَمَّلَهُ

والخدُّ منهُ الْحَيَاءُ كلَّلهُ   وبالنباتِ الْعِذَارِ حَلَّاهُ [3]

مَتَى يُوَافِي بِوَعْدِ مُكْرَبِهِ

\130أ\ مَتَى يُرَى الحبُّ مِنْ تَحَجُّبِهِ

مَتَى أُنَاجِيهِ مِنْ تَعَتُّبِهِ

مَتَى أَرَاهُ وَالطَّيْفُ مَالَ بِهِ   يَوْمًا إِلَى مَضْجَعِي وَأَلْقَاهُ [6]

لَوْ زَارَنِي أَحْمَدَ <الَّذِينَ سَعَوْا>

بِفُرْقَتِي ثُمَّ لِلْقُلُوبِ شَفَوْا

وَكَانَ مِن شَخْصِهِ الْوُشَاةُ رَأَوْا

وَكُنْتُ خَدّي لَهُ فَرَشْتُ وَلَوْ   بِالْهُدْبِ يَرْضَى كنَستُ مَمْشَاهُ [7]

كَمْ عَاذِلٍ زَادَ فِي الْمَلَامِ وَجَدَّ

وَلَا سَبِيلًا إِلَى السُّلُوِّ وَجَدْ

فَقُلْتُ وَالْقَلْبُ بِاللَّهِيبِ وَقَدْ

يَا قَاتَلَ اللهُ عَاذِلِي فَلَقَدْ   حَذَّرَنِي فِي الْهَوَى وَأَغْرَاهُ   [8]

Translation #347

a. He greets, and his face makes men alive again.

b. The lips awaken the thirst for his fire of love

c. and his saliva is pure sweetness on his front teeth.

I= [1] >For this gazelle of a herd points to a gloriously fragrant musk, may he (i.e., the gazelle/beloved) be blessed by God!<

a. O censor, stop your reproaches if

b. you want to get rid of someone whose heart burned with love for him (the gazelle),

c. and who has hidden his love-longing in his innermost being.

II= [5] >A gazelle of a herd, whose drinking place and pasture is in my eyes and in my innermost being (my last spark of life = *ḥušāšatī*).<

a. By God, the separation from him made the sorrow boil and

b. how much my affection for him grew in my heart!

c. How many spoke of him, and how many did he attract (lit.: deviate from the way)!

III= [2] >The sublime one has aligned his graceful stature evenly / and he created him as a temptation.<

a. Blessed is he who endowed him with beauty

b. and who sent him as a temptation for men,

c. and whose moonlike face completed the sky. [30]

IV= [3] >He crowned his cheeks with the redness of shame and adorned his cheeks with the plantlets.<

a. When does he finally hurry to keep his promise?

b. When does love finally show itself, when he always avoids the gaze?

c. How can I finally entrust myself to him, when he always shows hardness?

V= [6] >When do I see him and will his shadow be leading him toward my bed one day, so that I finally meet him?<

a. If he had visited me, "those who eagerly chased after" [Q 22:51; Q 34:5; Q 62:9] me in my pain of separation would have been extinguished

b. [… me in my pain of separation]. For then the hearts would be healed.

---

[30] This verse reads lit.: "The face – which the full moon in heaven – completed", but then it conveys a strange tautology.

c. Then the slanderers would finally end their rebuke (*or*: The slanderers used to see him from a distance).[31]

VI= [7] >So I bared my cheeks to him, and if he had given a sign with his eyelashes, I would have swept his way (?).<

a. How many censors strengthened their rebuke and became zealous

b. but no way to comfort (about his love spell) was found.

c. Thus I said, wherein the heart was kindled by the fiery passion:

VII= [8] >May God fight my censor, for he has warned me of love, and has thereby only encouraged it even more.<

The consequence of the change in verse order is that the focus of the motifs shifts to some extent, although Māmayh explicitly remains within the theme and genre of the poem:

Ibn Mulayk al-Ḥamawī

- praising of the beauty of the beloved and praising God for his creation (vv. 1–3)
- *taḫalluṣ* (v. 4)

---

[31] This verse VI [7 c] is not clear to me due to its wording and the variants. Either it is a final clause of the preceding verses (VI [a, b]) or a verse unrelated to these two, which is followed by verse VI [7]. The third hemistich in *taḫmīs* poems frequently follows the two preceding ones to conclude a given thought, or it is formulated as an expansion prefixing the subsequent *ṣadr*-verse.

- inaccessibility of the beloved youth (vv. 5–7)
- *recusatio* +a curse on the censor (v. 8)

Māmayh

- praising of the physiognomy (vv. I a–c)
- *recusatio*: defending his affection addressing the censor (vv. II a–c)
- praise of the beauty addressing God and his creation; love as a temptation (vv. III a–c IV a–c; vv. IV a–c taḫalluṣ)
- *accusatio*: complaints about the inaccessible beloved emphasizing the poet's forlornness with interrogative clauses (vv. V a–c)
- desired ways for deliverance and unification (vv. VI a–c)
- *recusatio*: a curse on the warning censor, who is the reason for being completely lost in love (vv. VII a–c)

Ibn Mulayk's *ghazal* has a moderately clear thematic structure, which Māmayh fans out in more minute terms. In doing so, he magnifies the pain and longing for love. While Ibn Mulayk does not mention the obligatory curse until the final verse, in the *taḫmīs* it is placed earlier and is given a more significant role for expressing the lost state of the lover. God remains the creator of the beloved's beauty in both poems, but in Māmayh's expansion, the aspect of temptation to which the lover had fallen prey is added.

The meter of the *ghazal* is *munsariḥ*. Except for the first *tafʿilah*, which Māmayh varies within the scope of poetic licenses, he accurately sticks to Ibn Mulayk's prosodic pattern, so that his own hemistichs flow naturally into Ibn Mulayk's melody without diminishing the accent in the *ṣadr*-verse with its incisive rhyme (*āhū*). Māmayh impressively manages to present both the 'new' (i.e., his own verses) and the 'old' in a very balanced way without trying to aesthetically outplay Ibn Mulayk's original.

Taḍmīn: a Stylistic Variation on a Theme

In the following examples of mimesis, the focus will be on *taḍmīn*, where it constitutes the poetic form of epigrams, and not on *taḍmīn* as a literary technique that frequently occurs in other types of poetry. The poet's motivation is similar to that of *taḫmīs*, as a stylistic exercise for variation, or, and this is different from *taḫmīs*, to challenge the original limit of the quoted verse to achieve a particularly striking effect of alienation. A further possibility is to bring an old verse back into poetic memory and compete with its poetic statement. Māmayh uses both verses/quotations that are not worn out in the *taḍmīn* tradition, but also those that have been quoted frequently in order to connect to this specific tradition and to stand out within it. Thus, the poet enters a dialogue at different communication levels: there is a dialogue from text to text, poet to poet, and the diachronic dialogue with the poetic tradition of a special verse, while on every level he is of course always in dialogue with the 'all-knowing' reader with a keen eye for detecting plagiarism. The following *muǧūn* epigram displays a *tawriyah* (double entendre)[32] with the polysemic use of the word *ḫalīl*:

[32] Where there is a *tawriyah*, the apparent meaning is set in front of round brackets, and the less obvious meaning(s!) are underlined within them. However, readers may perceive the 'apparent' and the 'less apparent' differently. Thus, the positions of the given meanings may also be changed.

[#520] وله مجُونٌ في اسم خليل [من الخفيف]

1 لَسْتُ أَنْسَى إِذْ نَامَ تَحْتِي خَلِيلٌ جَسَّ أَيْرِي رَآهُ أَمْرًا مَهُولَا

2 قَالَ ماذَا فَقُلْتُ فظٌّ غَلِيظٌ >لَا يُرَاعِي مِنَ[في/بين] الأَنَامِ خَلِيلَا<

Variants: 2. [فظٌّ]:فضّ/قِطٌّ; [مِنَ الأَنَامِ]: في/بين

I do not forget Ḫalīl, when he slept under me / he touched my penis that frightened him because of its size.

He said, what is that? I said: He is an incompliant crude one (or for *faḍḍ*: abrasive piercer), / "who does not care for Ḫalīl (a friend/a poor[33]) among people."

The epigram contains a proverbial *taḍmīn* (لا يُرَاعِي مِنَ الأَنَامِ خَلِيلَا) that is already adapted in the *Sīrat ʿAntarah*,[34] a text that belonged to the compulsory educational literature of the janissaries.[35] This same cento was

33 For this notion for *ḫalīl* see Ernst Trumpp: "Der Bedingungssatz im Arabischen", in: *Sitzungsberichte der Philosophisch-philologischen und historischen Classe der Königlichen bayerischen Akademie der Wissenschaften zu München. Vol. 2, 2 vols.* (München: Akademische Buchdruckerei von F. Straub, 1881), 2:372.

34 Verse 1–a in *Sīrat ʿAntarah b. Šaddād*, edition Turāṯ [repr. *Sīrat fāris fursān al-Ḥiǧāz Abī l-Fawāris ʿAntarah b. Šaddād: wa-hiya s-sīrah al-fāʾiqah al-ḥiǧāziyyah al-muštamilah ʿalā l-aḫbār al-aǧībah wa-l-anbāʾ al-ǧaliyyah*, 8 vols. (Beirut: al-Maktabah al-ʿIlmiyyah al-Ḥadīṯah, 1399/1979)] 8 vols. (Beirut: Dār al-Kutub al-ʿIlmiyyah, 1980], 3:162.

35 Zehra Öztürk: "Eğitim Tarihimizde Okuma Toplantarının Yeri ve Okunan Kitaplar", in: *Değerler Eğitimi Dergisi* 1 (2003), 141, and Lütfi Sezen: *Halk Edebiyatında Hamzanâmeler* (Ankara: Kültür Bakanlığı Yayınları, 1991), intr. VII, 18, 22, 42, 44.

used, for example, by Burhān ad-Dīn al-Qīrāṭī (d. 781/1379) in a mocking epigram for al-Ṣafadī (d. 764/1363), whose first name is Ḫalīl.[36] Māmayh also plunges into the subject by recontextualising the verse and by adding a daring allusion to the Quranic passage: *law kunta faẓẓan ġalīẓa l-qalbi* (Q 3:159).[37] Further, he signals and stresses the pun (*al-*)*anāmi* + *ḫalīl* of the cento with an equivocal but limping bi-conjunct *taǧnīs* in line 1–a with the words: *nāma … ḫalīl*.[38]

The next two examples display a *taḍmīn* with an often-quoted verse from al-Ṭuġrāʾī's *Lāmiyyāt al-ʿAǧam*: لِي أُسْوَةٌ بِانْحِطَاطِ الشَّمْسِ عَنْ زُحَلِ . Māmayh used the same cento twice in his *dīwān*. In #782 within a *ghazal*-epigram that displays a *Rangstreit* (dispute about rank) between the cheek and the birthmark. Māmayh inverts the poetic message to have it come out of the mouth of the birthmark, whereas in #1138, in a wine vs. coffee epigram, he asserts the original message, which comes out of the mouth of coffee:

36 Ibn Ḥiǧǧah: *Ḫizānat al-adab wa-ġāyat al-arab*, ed. Kawkab Diyāb, 5 vols. (Beirut: Dār Ṣādir, 2005), 4:410 (chapter on *tawriyah*). See also ʿIzz ad-Dīn al-Mawṣilī's (d. 789/1387) epigram with the same cento cited in ʿAlāʾ ad-Dīn ʿAlī b. ʿAbdallāh al-Ġuzūlī: *Maṭāliʿ l-budūr fī manāzil as-surūr*, ed. Saʿīd Maḥmūd at-Tiǧānī, 2 vols. (Beirut: Dār al-Kutub al-ʿIlmiyyah, 1438/2017), 1:486.

37 Q 3:159 (فَبِمَا رَحْمَةٍ مِّنَ اللَّهِ لِنتَ لَهُمْ وَلَوْ كُنتَ فَظًّا غَلِيظَ الْقَلْبِ لَانفَضُّوا مِنْ حَوْلِكَ ...) [transl. Pickthall] "It was by the mercy of [God] that thou wast lenient with them (O Muḥammad), for if thou hadst been stern and fierce of heart they would have dispersed from round about thee."

38 For these *taǧnīs* forms see Pierre Cachia: *The arch rhetorician or the schemer's skimmer: A handbook of late Arabic badīʿ drawn from ʿAbd al-Ġanī an-Nābulsī's* Nafaḥāt al-azhār ʿalā nasamāt al-asḥār, *summarized and systematized* (Wiesbaden: Harrassowitz, 1998), nrs. 29, 30 and 31.

[#782] وقال من الاستعارة [من البسيط]

1 لَمَّا تَبَاهَتْ عَلَى الجَنَّاتِ وَجْنَتُهُ   قَالَتْ تَرَكْتُ وُرُودَ الرَّوْضِ فِي خَجَلِ

2 وَأَسْوَدُ الخَالِ إِنْ يَعْلُو عَلَى شَفَتِي   >لِي أُسْوَةٌ بِانْحِطَاطِ الشَّمْسِ عَنْ زُحَلِ<

When the beauty of its cheek competed with the gardens, it said, "You have left the rose in shame."

Then the black of the birthmark, as it rose above the lips, said: "I know an example where the sun descends before Saturn."

[#1138] وله أيضًا مضمنًا [من البسيط]

1 قد قالت القهوة الحمراء وافتخرتْ   كم قد ملكت ملوكَ العصرِ والدُّولِ

2 وقهوةُ القِدرِ إن قِدْرًا عليّ [علتْ]   >لي أُسوةٌ بانحطاط الشمس عن زحلِ<

The red coffee (i.e., wine) said proudly: "The rulers of how many dynasties and epochs have I ruled.

And the pot wine (i.e., coffee), (even) when it rises above me in its rank then, "I know an example where the sun sets (descends) before Saturn."

With the verse >السَّيْفُ أَصْدَقُ أَنْبَاءً مِنَ الْكُتُبِ< (The sword is more truthful than books) Abū Tammām succeeded in creating one of the most imposing entry verses of a *qaṣīdah* ever. Many poets labored over this verse both in a *taḍmīn* and in numerous poetic imitations on the given motif (sword vs. *qalam* scripture/fig. speech).[39] Poetic grandees such as Ibn Nubātah even incorporated this verse three times into their poems.[40] Regardless of its popularity, however, this verse is rarely found in epigrams, perhaps because of its brilliance and superiority, but it appears much more frequently in longer *qaṣīdahs*. Māmayh belongs with poets such as Šayḫ aš-Šuyūḫ Ḥamāh (Šaraf ad-Dīn [Ibn Rifāʾ] al-Anṣārī, d. 662/1264), Ibn Mulayk al-Ḥamawī (d. 917/1512)[41] and ʿAbdallāh b. al-Faqīh aṣ-Ṣūfī (Ibn Aḥmad Maḫramat al-Yamanī, d. 972/1565)[42] among those who integrated the verse into an epigram. Formally, the verse moves from its original position I-a into the *ʿağuz*-verse of the epigram, so that the poetic message of the epigram must culminate in something which it had been originally started with. In Šayḫ aš-Šuyūḫ's epigram the verse leads to a parable concerning the superiority of the Quran over previous scriptures. In Ibn Mulayk, the verse serves as a *faḫr* of one's strength and as a warning to enemies. ʿAbdallāh al-Ṣūfī's *ghazal* epigram uses the verse as a verdict of fate that separated him from the beloved. Māmayh places the famous verse within the frequently employed motif of comparing the cutting glances of the beloved to the cutting edge of the sword.

---

39 Al-Anṣārī composed a *taḍmīn* epigram for his šayḫ Sayfaddīn al-Āmidī with a *tawriyah* on *sayf*. The *taḍmīn* is used allegorically in combination with the prophet's praise, see Ibn Ḥiğğah: *Ḫizānat al-adab*, 4:148.

40 The *taḍmīn* verse occurs in longer poems. See Ğamāl ad-Dīn Muḥammad b. Muḥammad Ibn Nubātah al-Miṣrī (686–768/1287–1366): *Dīwān Ibn Nubātah al-Miṣrī*, ed. Muḥammad al-Qalqīlī (Cairo/Miṣr: Maṭbaʿat at-Tamaddun, 1323/1905), 22, 41 and 52.

41 Ibn Mulayk al-Ḥamawī: *Dīwān al-nafaḥāt al-adabiyyah min al-zahrāt al-Ḥamawiyyah*, ed. Isrāʾ Aḥmad Fawzī al-Hayb (Damascus: Manšūrāt al-Hayʾah al-ʿĀmmah as-Sūriyah li-l-Kutub, 2010), 240.

42 al-ʿAydarūs, *an-Nūr as-sāfir ʿan aḫbār al-qarn al-ʿāšir*, eds. Aḥmad Ḥālū et al. (Beirut: Dār Ṣādir, 2001), 378–84, and 381 (epigram).

[#909] وله تضمينٌ أيضًا [من البسيط]

1 مُذْ رَاسَلَتْنِي سُيُوفُ اللَّحْظِ وَاشْتَهَرَتْ   وَحَارَبَتْنِي وَدَمْعِي سَاحَ مِنْ حَرَبِي

2 صَدَّقْتُ قَوْلَ الَّذِي قَالَ مِنْ قِدَمٍ   <السَّيْفُ أَصْدَقُ أَنْبَاءً مِنَ الْكُتُبِ>

When glances sharp like swords unsheathed targeted and attacked me, out of angst I cried.

I came to believe the truthfulness of what one long past said: "The sword is more truthful than books."

Māmayh transfers the scene into a classical *ghazal* epigram but uses the war lexis as a *tawǧīh* to harmonize with and recall the initial context of the verse. The cento, already announced in II-a and into which the poetic message culminates, serves as the textual confirmation of his defeat (i.e., love pain).

Another poignant *ghazal* epigram is combined with a quotation from the *ḥadīṯ* (أنَّ أبوابَ الجنَّةِ تحتَ ظلالِ السُّيوفِ *The gates of Paradise are under the shadows of the swords*).[43]

[#921] وَأَيْضًا [بَحْرُ السَّرِيعِ]

1 أَفْدِي غَزَالًا خَدُّهُ جَنَّةٌ   مِنَ الْبَهَا وَالْحُسْنِ زَادَتْ صُنُوفْ

2 مَنْ رَامَهَا مَاتَ شَهِيدًا بِهَا   لِأَنَّهَا <تَحْتَ ظِلَالِ السُّيُوفْ> [حديث]

43 This *taḍmīn* verse also occurs as the final verse of a seven-liner by Ibn Nubātah: *Dīwān*, 462.

> I would give everything for the gazelle, whose cheeks are like the heavenly garden. And its qualities (صنوف various sorts, or صنوف عسكرية، طوائف عسكرية, military units) increased because of her beauty and magnificence.
>
> Whoever sought for her, died as a martyr for her, "because [she is] under the shadows of the swords [there is the Paradise]."

The cento is unmarked and incomplete, but already prepared in I-a (here: *ǧannah*) and then rendered in a causal phrase (*li-annahā* …). Since the gazelle and paradise were already equated in I-a, the message of the *ḥadīṯ* is valid for both: for the Paradise, that cannot be reached without effort or martyrdom, and for the beloved, that is only to be won with a heavy sacrifice.

In addition to the written testimonies, proverbs also served as quotations in the epigram, to connect the truth based on common sense (or experience) with varying circumstances and so either to give emphasis to it or to reverse the truth conveyed in it. Māmayh inserts such a cento in the setting of a drinking scene. It is the proverbial saying: أَلْف دُقْدُق ولا سلام عليكم which to my knowledge addresses the visitor and means not to barge in (i.e, the direction is from outside to inside) somewhere without knocking, even if a thousand times. Here Māmayh, reverses the direction (inside to outside) by putting this cento in the mouth of a boon companion, to recall the censors knocking at the door but telling them not to burst into the tavern, even when the door would not be opened (*lā salām ʿalaykum*):

[#1068] وله تضمين [بحر الخفيف]

1 إِنْ سَكِرْتُمْ وَكُنْتُمْ فِي مَقَامْ لَا تَخَافُوا وُصُولَ شَرٍّ إِلَيْكُمْ

2 فَاغْلِقُوا الْبَابَ وَانْشِدُوا مَنْ أَتَاكُمْ <أَلْفُ دُقْدُقٍ وَلا سَلَامُ عَلَيْكُمْ>[المثل]

Variants: 2. [دقدق]: طقطق

If you are drunken and you are in a tavern, do not fear that something bad will come.

Just close the doors and recite to those coming: "a thousand knock-knocks and no greeting!"

Māmayh also addressed his contemporaries with such epigrams. The one who occupied him the most was probably al-ʿUqaydī, since six entire mocking epigrams in the *dīwān* are dedicated to this so-called poet-pretender:

[#1227] وله أَيضًا فيه [من الوافر]

1 أَلَا يَا مُدَّعٍ مَا لَيْسَ فِيهِ وَيَلْحَنُ كُلَّ وَقْتٍ فِي النِّظَامِ

2 فَنَظْمُكَ مِثْلُ شَكْلِكَ مِثْلُ دِسْتٍ سُخَامٌ فِي سُخَامٍ فِي سُخَامِ

O you poor pretender who talks nonsense all the time in poetry.

So I composed for you, something which is similar to your shape of a cooking pot: smut, over smut, over smut (*suḫām* fig. nonsense).

I found no evidence for the phrase (سُخَامٌ فِي سُخَامٍ فِي سُخَامِ) in II-b in poetry or proverb collections, but it seems to be a response to a lampoon once directed at Māmayh by another contemporary poet Qānṣūh al-Ǧarkasī, in which he compared Māmayh to a black mulberry.[44] Qānṣūh's verse ends with the phrase: black (in) over black (in) over black.[45] Thus, both poets differently adapt an older tradition of the stylistic figure of *taṭrīz* (reverbation).[46]

Al-ʿUqaydī was attacked again with a quotation that is a known verse but of uncertain origin. It occurs already in Ibn Ḥiǧǧah's *Ḫizānat al-adab* as a quotation and occupies the whole verse II (a–b):[47]

[#1226] \279أ\ وله أيضا فيه هجو [من الطويل]

1 أَلَا أَيُّهَا الدَّحْمُورُ فِي كُلِّ فَنِّهِ   وَمَنْ قَدْ غَدَا فِي الكِبْرِيَا وَهْوَ صَاغِرُ

2 <إِذَا كُنْتَ لَا تَدْرِي سِوَى الوَزْنِ وَحْدَهُ   فَقُلْ أَنَا وَزَّانٌ وَمَا أَنَا شَاعِرُ>
[البيت المعروف]

44 Black mulberry (here *at-tūt aš-Šāmī*) probably refers to an ingredient for black ink.

45 Ibn Ayyūb: *Kitab ar-rawḍ al-ʿāṭir*, 2:817 (verse: *suʿādun fī suʿādin fī suʿād*).

46 For *taṭrīz* (sometimes also *tawšīʿ*) see Ibn Abī l-Iṣbaʿ al-Miṣrī: *Taḥrīr at-taḥbīr fī ṣināʿat aš-šiʿr wa-n-naṯr wa-bayān iʿǧāz l-Qurʾān*, ed. Ḥifnī Muḥammad Šaraf (Cairo: al-Maǧlis al-Aʿlā li-š-Šuʾūn al-Islāmiyyah, Laǧnat Iḥyā at-Turāṯ al-Islāmī, [1963]), 314–5, and Ibn Ḥiǧǧah: *Ḫizānat al-adab*, 96–7. Regarding the usage of this figure to denote colors the literary compendia refer to an anecdote and to verses composed by Abū Nuwās, Abū l-ʿAtāhiyah and Diʿbil in a poetic contest. Each of them was describing a color of the threefold robes worn by a beautiful slave girl (Aḥmad ibn Muḥammad al-Anṣārī al-Yamanī aš-Širwānī: *Kitāb nafḥat al-Yaman fī mā yazūlu bi-ḏikrihi aš-šaǧan* (Miṣr: al-Maṭbaʿah al-ʿĀmirah aš-Šarqīyah, 1305 [1888]), 31. – I thank Thomas Bauer for pointing out these references.

47 Ibn Ḥiǧǧah: *Ḫizānat al-adab*, 3:523.

This little donkey in all his confused speech (lit.: art), and who acts in dull pride while he is contemptible.

>If you are just able to master only a single meter, then say "I am a meterist," not a poet!<

Taḫmīs #347 (ر)

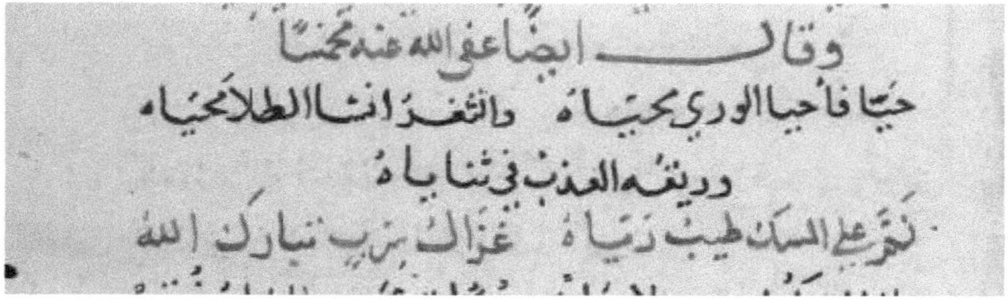

وقال ـــــ ايضا عفى الله عنه مخمسا

حيا فاحيا الورى بحياه   دا الثغر انسا الطلا محياه

وريقه العذب في ثناياه

نمّ على المسك طيب رياه   غزال سرب تبارك الله

--------- صدر   --------- صدر

--------- صدر

(------- صدر   ------- عجز)

#1013 Burdah-Taḫmīs (خ)

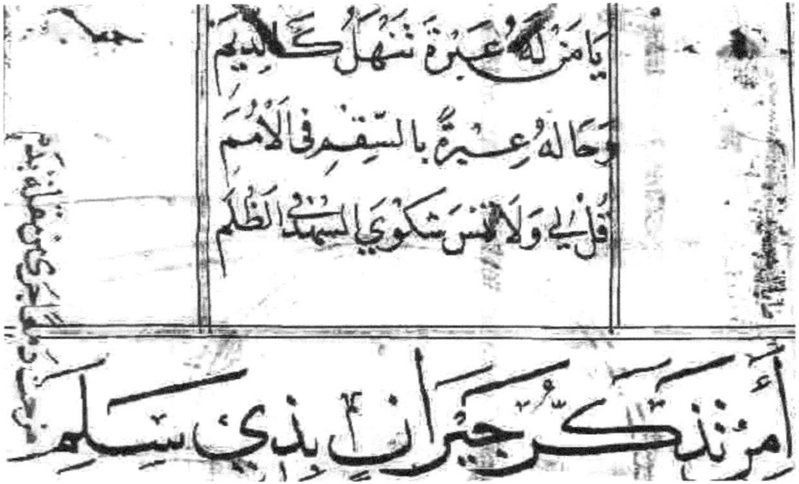
يا من له عبرة تنهل كالديم
وحاله عبرة بالسقم في الأمم
قل لي ولا تنس شكوى السهد في الظلم
أمن تذكر جيران بذي سلم
مزجت دمعا جرى من مقلة بدم

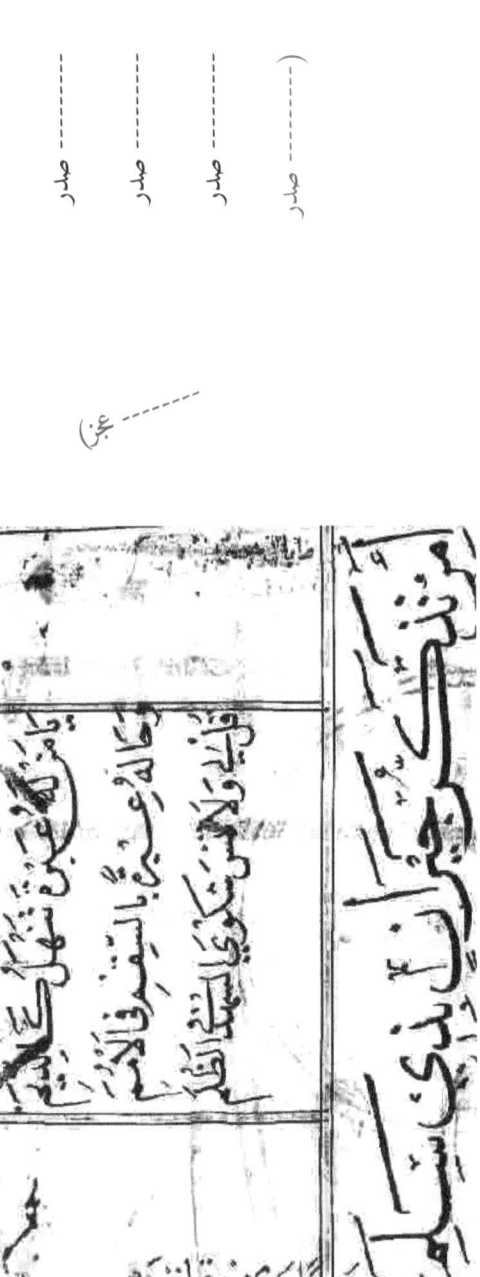

--------- صدر

--------- صدر

--------- صدر

(--------- صدر

عجز ---------

Taḫmīs #347 (ق)

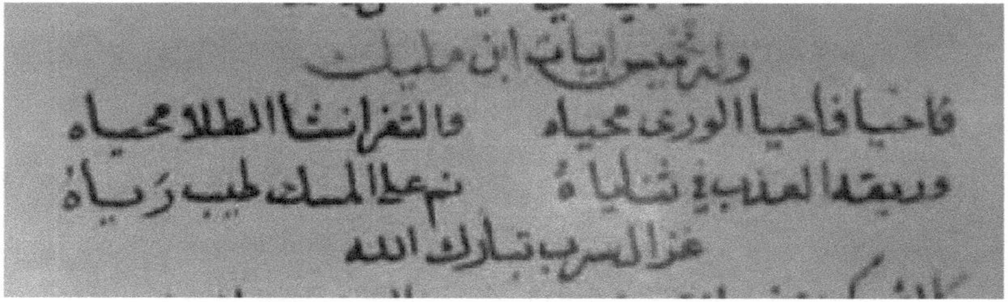
ولہ تخميس ابيات ابن مليك
فاحيا فاحيا الورى محياه   فالثغر انشا الطلا محياه
وريقه العذب في ثناياه   نم على المسك طيب رياه
عز الرب تبارك الله

صدر --------- صدر ---------

صدر --------- (صدر ---------

(عجز ---------

 # 347 (ع)

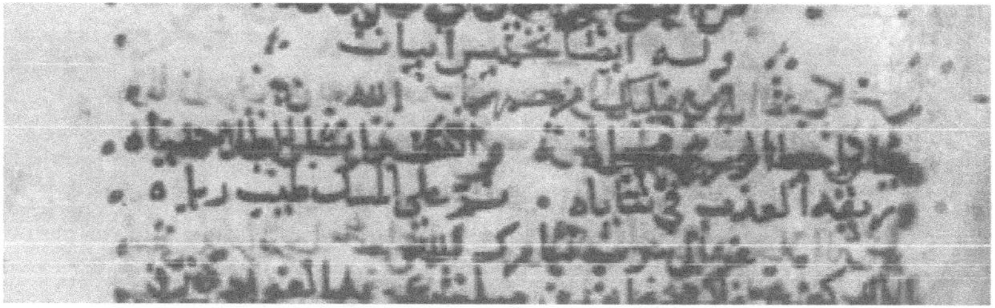
وله ايضا تخميس ابيات
وريقه العذب في ثناياه   نم على المسك طيب رياه

Taḫmīs #347 (ز)

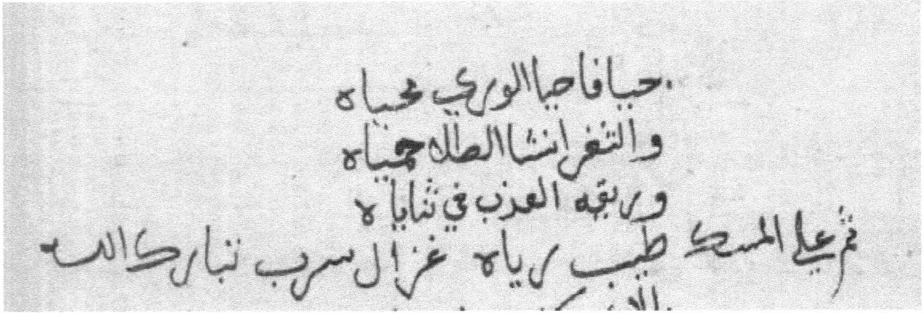

حيا فاحيا الورى محياه
والثغر انشا الطلا حمياه
وريقه العذب في ثناياه
ثم على المسك طيب رياه غزال سرب تبارك الله

#347 (د)

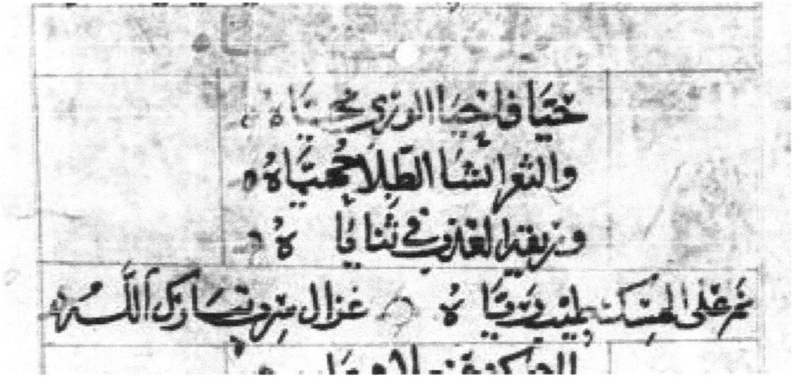

حيا فاحيا الورى محياه
والثغر انشا الطلا حمياه
وريقه العذب في ثناياه
ثم على المسك طيب رياه غزال سرب تبارك الله

صدر ---------

صدر ---------

صدر ---------

(------- صدر ------- عجز)

The Modern

The Modern

So far, we have concentrated on Māmayh's poetic approach to the past in some traditional poetic genres. Among the newer themes and poetic forms are chronograms, *mulammaʿāt* (as multilingual poems), nonclassical meters like *d̲ūbayts* and *silsilah*; several poetic forms in the vernacular (*azǧāl* and most of his *mawāliyā*) and his *mukayyifāt* poems, mainly those about *barš*, *ḥašīš*, *afyūn*, and *qahwah*. As a virtuoso, Māmayh also had a special predilection for ludic, lettristic, and phonetic word games. One would be inclined to call him an ecstatic graphophile if there were not just as many examples of classical poetry in his oeuvre. In any case, he offers the reader a spectacular array of genre-transcending composition and decomposition techniques with letters that leave the realm of the medial and achieve greatness in their own right.[48] Such lettristic games are common in many different poetic traditions and languages. Like the Arabs, the Persians excelled in these techniques, and they flourished in European literary history, especially in the Baroque period. The *Zaum*-language of the Russian Futurists, the literature of Dadaism, and Oulipo (acronym: L'Ouvroir de Littérature Potentielle), an international group of writers who

---

[48] Lachmann ("Kalligraphie, Arabeske, Phantasma", 456) states the following on the role of letters as autonomous signs fluctuating between iconography, magic and semantics:

> "When letters as multi-referential signs act as autonomous individual signs, they follow the logic of combination and permutation, which creates crypto-semantic paths in word and text, they gain a visual profile in their respective, pictorially interpretable or self-sufficient sign form, or they unfold words out of their sounds. Letter magicians and calligraphers, lettrists and abecedary artists tame and unbind the semantic-somatic potential of the alphabets and inscribe it in orders of the hidden sense, the ornament, the image, and the lexicon."

create works in which they follow specific, self-imposed rules, can be considered the modern offshoots of this style of literary expression.

Many of the prevalent techniques of constrained writing also appear in the *dīwān* of Māmayh. These are writing devices bound by conditions that forbid certain things or impose a pattern. There are poems with dotted or undotted letters and with alternating punctuation or words and entire lines alternating with different devices:

Constrained Writing

I *aš-šiʿr al-manqūṭ* (*al-ḫālī, al-mušakkal, al-muʿǧam*): dotted letters;[49]

II *aš-šiʿr al-ʿāṭil* (*al-muhmal*): undotted letters;[50]

III *aš-šiʿr al-arqaṭ*: alternating dotted and undotted letters;[51]

IV *aš-šiʿr al-aḫyaf*: alternating words with dotted and undotted letters;

V *aš-šiʿr al-mulammaʿ*: either a poem with alternating sequence of verses with techniques (I–IV); or a multilingual poem with alternating lines in different languages;

---

49 *Dīwān* Māmayh, e.g., poems: #37; #434; #492; #493; #526; #553; #606; #1123.

50 *Dīwān* Māmayh, e.g., poems: #36; #37; #127; #168; #382; #384; #385; #432; #433; #434; #492; #493; #494; #496; #513; #553; #603; #605; #627; #704; #705; #718; #991; #1063; #1065; #1123; #1149; #1150.

51 *Dīwān* Māmayh, e.g., poems: #36 (?); #434; #1057; #492; #455; #553.

VI *aš-šiʿr al-maḥbūk*: the beginning and the end of a verse with the same letter or a subset of letters;

VII *aš-šiʿr al-muṭṭariz*: acrostics, bipartite acrostics (acrostich+ telestich); multiple acrostics with e.g. personal names;[52]

VIII *aš-šiʿr al-muqaṭṭaʿ*: letters (أ,د,ذ,ر,ز,و) not connected to the letter following them vs. or alternating *aš-šiʿr al-muwaṣṣal/al-muṭṭaṣil*: connected letters;

IX *maǧmaʿ al-baḥrayn*: polymetrical poems: alternating meters within a single poem by altering the inflection;

X Alliteration or tautograms, in which every word must start with the same letter (or subset of letters);

XI *abǧadiyyah*: abecedarius (in which the first letter of every word, strophe or verse follows the order of the letters in the alphabet);

XII Reverse-lipograms: each word must contain a particular letter;

XIII … palindromes, pangrams, riddles, chronograms, etc.

Māmayh uses such devices to a great extent in the newer types of poetry (*al-funūn as-sabʿa*), especially in *zaǧal* and *mawāliyā* poems – and through it contributes to the extension of the poetics in these genres, i.e., to the '*badīʿ*ization of the vernacular'. However, the tendency to permeate vernacular genres with this kind of ornate speech and figures of *badīʿ* was

[52] *Dīwān* Māmayh, e.g., poems: #272; #682; #683; #1123; #1219 (?).

already established in the time of Ṣafī ad-Dīn al-Ḥillī (d. ca. 749/1348).[53] Such literary techniques create an intermediality between the spoken and the visual and thus embed the newer genres into the aesthetic tradition of classical poetics.

A speciality of Māmayh is his acrostics (#682), a poetic device in which the initial letters of each line, when read vertically, spell out a word or phrase. Māmayh not only uses multiple acrostics, but also includes examples with an alternating direction: bottom-up and top-down.

[#682]

1	عَذَّبْتَ قَلْبِي بِطَرْفٍ زَايِدِ الْوَسَنِ	وَفِي مُحَيَّاكَ شَهْدٌ غَرْسُهُ دُرَرُ
2	لَوْ جُدْتَ لِي بِرُضَابٍ زَانَهُ لَعَسٌ	لَمَّا شَكَوْتُ الظَّمَا يَا أَيُّهَا الْقَمَرُ
3	يَكْفِيكَ أَنَّ الْمُعَنَّى بَاتَ فِي تَرَحٍ	يَذُوبُ شَوْقًا وَنَارُ الشَّوْقِ تَسْتَعِرُ
	‘Alī ↓ ↑Ḥasan	Walī ↓ ↑‘Umar

Another extraordinary poem is Māmayh's *Abecedarius* (#1055), a special type of acrostic in which the first letter of every word, verse, or strophe

53 On the developments in the arts of the *zağal*, see Wilhelm Hoenerbach: "Zwei Studien zur spanisch-arabischen Literatur", in: *ZDMG* 141 (1991), 253–80, and see also Margret Larkin: "The Dust of the Master. A Mamlūk-Era 'Zajal' by Ḫalaf al-Ghubārī", in: *Quaderni di Studi Arabi, N.S.* 2 (2007), 11–29 for the famous *zağğāl* al-Ġubārī to whom Māmayh frequently refers to in his own *zağals* and boasts of having surpassed him.

follows the order of the letters in the alphabet.[54] Known since antiquity, this device appears in the Hebrew Bible, in all languages of the Islamic world, and in Turkish is known as *Elifnâmes*. In Russian and in Western literature, it appears particularly in hymns, prophecies, and prayers as a meditative and also as a mnemonic technique. Māmayh composed such a poem (31 verses) in praise of the Prophet, following the alphabet. It has also other self-imposed constraints, as besides the complicated (*-ānī*)-end-rhyme, Māmayh imposes several internal rhymes with the letters *alif*, and *yāʾ*. These horizontally cross the vertical alphabetical line and together give an impression of a woven fabric with a symmetrical stitching. Similar to the biblical "I am the Alpha and the Omega", these letters (*alif* and *yāʾ*) are the first and the last letters of the Arabic alphabet, reflecting the Islamic belief that the prophet Muḥammad is the reason for creation and is the last messenger.

Coffee Poems

According to Ibn Ayyūb, Māmayh loved to get married and was addicted to marijuana (here: *al-ḥašīšah al-ḫaḍrāʾ*), so much so that one saw him more often 'high' than sober.[55] Māmayh, not only consumed intoxicants,

---

54 For example, verse 2 (note, that the names of the letters are an integral part of this poem and its prosody. In some mss. the letter names were omitted, which makes the meter defective):

بَاءٌ بَدَا مَدْحِي لِأَحْمَدَ ذِي الْهُدَى ... وَبِهِ غَدًا أَنْجُو مِنَ النِّيرَانِ

55 Šaraf ad-Dīn Ibn Ayyūb: "at-Taḏkirah [al-Ayyūbiyyah]", MS aẓ-Ẓāhiriyyah 7814, Damascus, fol. 129b:

"He was not inclined towards handsome boy servants (*al-ġilmān*) but he loved women and hence he married and divorced a lot. He used *al-ḥašīšah al-ḫaḍrāʾ* on most of the days, moreover every day." Ibn Ayyūb omits his remark on Māmayh's *ḥāšīš* addiction in his *ar-Rawḍ al-ʿāṭir*.

but he also wrote numerous poems about them (*al-mukayyifāt*)[56], mainly about coffee. The poems stretch across all poetic (vernacular and classical) forms and the following overview shows the occurrences of these themes in his *dīwān*:

> *qahwah*: #63 (?); #167; #241; #475; #476; #777; #804; #807; #808; #855; #933; #988; #993; #998; #1039; #1044; #1048; #1049; #1138; #1150; #1116; #1203; #1230; #1295; #1319; #1323
>
> *barš*; #555; #746; #890; #1049; #1148; #1150; #1152
>
> *ḥašīš*: #512; #610; #611; #631; #696; #997; #1048; #1049; #1150 (*afyūn*); #1152 (*afyūn*); #1156; #1273; #1274

At the time Māmayh wrote his poems, coffee, and with it the coffee house, had only been known in Syria for a few decades. Since its first appearance, however, there had been heated debates about the legality of the new beverage.[57] The city had split into two factions, whose respective spokesmen argued for and against coffee in treatises, *fatwās*, and poems. On the side of the opponents to coffee was the Šāfiʿīte scholar and *ḫaṭīb* Yūnus al-ʿĪṯāwī (898–ca. 987/1492–1579), whose letters to the imperial capital was largely responsible for Sulaymān I (r. 926–74/1520–66)

56 The *mukayyifāt* include poems about coffee, *barš*, *ḥašīš* and opium.

57 According to Ibn Ayyūb's (d. 1003/1594) account, coffee was already known in Damascus in the 910s and had already prompted writings and *fatwās* both for and against it (Ibn Ayyūb: *Kitab ar-rawḍ al-ʿāṭir*, 2:1100–03, see also 2:1092–99 with excerpts of *fatwās*). The introduction of the coffee houses (*ḥānūt*, pl. *ḥawānīt*, *bayt al-qahwah* or *al-maqāhī*) in Damascus is dated by al-Arnāʾūṭ to 947/1536 (Muḥammad M. al-Arnāʾūṭ: *Min at-tārīḫ aṯ-ṯaqāfī li-l-qahwah wa-l-maqāhī* (Beirut: Ǧadāwil, 2012), 38, see also 18–30 and 37–39).

decreeing the closure of coffee houses.[58] The group of proponents was represented by none other than the master Māmayhs, Abū l-Fatḥ al-Mālikī (d. 975/1567),[59] who himself was known for his excessive consumption of *barš*.[60]

In this example, the old and more venerable wine is contrasted with the young, highly popular coffee, as they have to share the same name:

[#855] هجوٌ في القهوة [بحر الطويل]

1 سَمِعْتُ لِسَانَ الحَالِ مِنْ قَهْوَةِ الطَّلَا تَقُولُ هَلُمّوا واسْمَعُوا نَصَّ أَخْبَارِي

2 أَبِسْمِي تَسَمَّتْ قَهْوَةُ البُنِّ فِي الْمَلَا وَلَكِنَّهَا لَمْ تَحْكِ [فعلا] خِمَارِي

3 فَمِنْ كِذْبِهَا قَدْ سَوَّدَ الحَقُّ وَجْهَهَا وَعَذَّبَهَا بَعْدَ الإِهَانَةِ بِالنَّارِ

I heard the *qahwah* of grapes (wine) saying: Come on and listen to what I have to say.

Has the coffee of beans taken my name publicly? Although her hangover (veil) does not resemble mine.

Because of her lie, God has blackened her face and punished her for defamation with hell (fire).

58 al-Arnā'ūṭ: *Min at-tārīḫ aṯ-ṯaqāfī li-l-qahwah*, 39 and Ibn Ayyūb: *Kitab ar-rawḍ al-ʿāṭir*, 2:1092–93; Abū l-Fatḥ's biography, idem, 2:898–909.

59 Ibn Ayyūb: *Kitab ar-rawḍ al-ʿāṭir*, 2:898–907 et passim. On the illustrious poetic polemic on coffee between him, al-ʿĪṯāwī, and other poets see al-Arnā'ūṭ: *Min at-tārīḫ aṯ-ṯaqāfī li-l-qahwah*, 74–103 et passim.

60 Ahmet Halil Güneş: *Das Kitāb ar-rauḍ al-ʿāṭir des Ibn-Aiyūb. Damaszener Biographien des 10./16. Jahrhunderts* (Berlin: Schwarz-Verlag, 1971), 68.

In another poem, Māmayh reverses the contrast. Here, the coffee, a beverage in its early heyday, boasts itself over the time-honored wine.

[#808] وفيه [بحر البسيط]

1 غَابَ السُّرُورُ وَعَنَّا غَابَ سَاقِينَا

وَرَاحَ مَنْ كَانَ بِالْبُشْرَى يُلَاقِينَا

2 وَقَلَّ مِنْ شُرْبِ كَأسِ الأُنْسِ رَاجِينَا

وَقَهْوَةُ الْبُنِّ قَالَتْ بِالْفَنَا جِينَا [بالفناء جئنا]

Our joy left us because our wine pourer left;

and because the one is gone, who used to meet us with glad tidings.

So, those companions with whom we shared our cups became less,

and the coffee said: (You know!) We came here only in porcelain cups (<u>transitory</u>).

If the last sentence is read as "porcelain cup", the antithesis to the previously mentioned "wine cup" becomes clear. However, this juxtaposition is not equally weighted. The wine takes up three lines, whereas the coffee is given only one line to defend itself. Thus, the coffee's speech must be incisive enough to outweigh the wine's merits. The reader may settle for the antithesis and move on to the next poem. However, hidden behind an astute pun, Māmayh gives the coffee more to say than just a verse length. By splitting the plural of *finǧān* (*fanāǧīn*[a]) into *bi-l-fanā*ʾ + coll. *ǧīnā* (for *ǧiʾnā*) he creates a bi-conjunct equivocal paronomasia (*ǧinās at-*

tawriyah),[61] that shows that the semantic layers of the epigram have not been exhausted. Coming from the tongue of coffee, the phrase (*We came here only transitory*) echoes a tone of pure sarcasm toward wine. The rhyme word has the 1st person plural (*ǧīnā*/*ǧi'nā*), so that the verse must be valid for both (coffee and wine). The last verse then reveals an attitude of cynicism, through which the coffee also refers to its own demise as the consumption of coffee was notoriously controversial.[62]

One outstanding composition is a *mawāliyā* (#1150) of 108 verses that displays his artistry in various stylistic figures in the vernacular. Māmayh alters the rhyme in every fourth line, as in proper *mawāliyā*.[63] The register of speech shifts considerably, from elaborate phrases (at the beginning and end of the poem) to coarse slang. Briefly, the main points of this poem are as follows: The topic is the closure of coffee houses in the year 966/1558. Māmayh opens with a lengthy city praise portraying the tranquil life of Damascus, its pleasant gardens, with people enjoying a cultivated urban setting with wine taverns as a symbol of the good old days

61 Cachia: *The arch rhetorician*, no. 23.

62 On the history of coffee and the emerging coffeehouse-culture in detail, see Ralf S. Hattox: *Coffee and Coffeehouses. The Origins of a Social Beverage in Medieval Near East* (Seattle/London: University of Washington Press, [3]1996); Eminegül Karababa and Güliz Ger: "Early Modern Ottoman Coffeehouse Culture and the Formation of the Consumer Subject", in: *Journal of Consumer Research* 37 (2011), 737–60 and Maḥmūd Mufliḥ al-Bakr: *al-Qahwah al-'arabiyyah fī l-mawrūṯ wa-l-adab as-ša'bī* (Beirut: Bīsān li-n-Našr wa-t-Tawzī' wa-l-I'lām 1995). On how coffee and the closure of coffeehouses was reflected in Arabic poetry see Nurettin Ceviz: "Kahvenin İslâm Dünyasına Girişi ve Arap Edebiyatında Ele Alınışı", in: *EKEV Akademi Dergisi* 18 (2004), 343–56, esp. 347.

63 Pierre Cachia: "The Egyptian Mawwāl", in: *Journal of Arabic Literature* 8 (1977), 77–103, Riḍā Muḥsin Ḥammūd al-Qurayšī: *al-Funūn aš-ši'riyya ġayr al-mu'raba: al-mawāliyā* (Baghdad: al-Maktabah al-Fūlklūriyyah, 1976).

(lines 9–26). Then, with the opening of coffeehouses, the newcomers *barš*[64] and coffee disturbed the tranquillity and led to a moral decline (lines 27–68). Both the musicality of the *mawāliyā* and the switching of linguistic registers – to match the speakers' sociolect – vividly depict the various stages of degeneration, underline the situation in formal and linguistic aspects, and even allow us to assume that this poem was recited in public.

[#1150] وهذا الحِمْل المَوَّال عمِلَه حين وردَ المرسوم بإِبْطال القهوة سنة 966

جَاءتْ شَبِيهَ غُرَابِ البِينِ ذِي القَهْوَهْ
فَابْطَلُوهَا وَفِيهَا أُنْفِذَتْ دَعْوَهْ
وَكَانَتِ النَّاسُ فَوْقَ المَرْجَةِ الخَضْرَهْ
تَشْرَبْ كُؤُوسَ الهَنَا بِالخَمْرَةِ الحَمْرَهْ

64 *Barš*, turc. *berş*, is the name for several popular drug mixtures based on opium. A special *barš*-mixture, consumed copiously by the "intelligentsia" was invented by ar-Raḥīkī (d. 1546). On Raḥīkī's *barš*-mixture and its ingredients see Benedek Péri: "A Janissary's Son Turned Druggist and His Highly Successful Designer Drug in 16th–17th Century", in: *Osmanlı İstanbulu IV*, eds. Feridun M. Emecen et al. (İstanbul: 29 Mayıs Üniversitesi Yayınları, 2016), 643–54; Murat Uluskan: "İstanbul'da Bir Afyonlu Macun İşletmesi: Berş-i Rahîkî Macunhanesi (1783–1831)", in: *Türk Kültürü İncelemeleri Dergisi* 29 (2013), 77–106. Gelibolulu ʿAlī provides a vivid account of some aspects of leisure culture in Ottoman society in his days (Mustafa Âli Gelibolulu: *The Ottoman Gentlemen of the sixteenth Century, Mustafa ʿAli's* "Tables of Delicacies Concerning the Rules of Social Gatherings [Mevāʾidü'n-nefāʾis fī ḳavāʿidi'l-mecālis]", trad. Douglas Brookes (Cambridge [Mass.]: Harvard University, 2003), esp. 50–54, 103, 111 on *barš* and other narcotics, and 129–133 on coffeehouses, wine and *boza* taverns).

31 وَاليَوْمَ بِالبَرْشِ أَضْحَوْا [أصبحوا] يكَسِرُوا الصُّفْرَه

32 وَيَشْرَبُوا القَهْوَةَ السُّودَا عَلَى بُكْرَه

This is a *mawāliyā* (a load of *mawwāl*), which he composed when the coffeehouses were abolished by a decree in 966/[1558]:

Then came the separation boding raven-like coffee

which they abolished and enforced the decree on her (i.e., coffee).

Once the people were (used to enjoy life) on green pastureland,[65]

drinking cups of felicity filled with red wine.

But nowadays with *barš*, they started to dishonor the banquet table,

and they drink the black coffee already in the morning.

To attest to this decline, Māmayh includes a lengthy tale of this issue describing the disgraceful habits of drugged men in the coffee houses:

.49 وَذَا يُغَنِّي وَذَا خَارِجْ وَذَا دَاخِلْ

.50 وَذَا بِدَعْوَى الحَقِيقَهْ خَاضَ فِي البَاطِلْ

---

65 *Al-marğah al-ḫaḍrah* (*al-ḫaḍrā'*!) alludes here also to the toponym in Damascus *Maydān al-Aḫḍar*, also called *Maydān al-Marğah*. It encloses the recreational place *al-Ğabhah*. See Qutaybah aš-Šihābī: *Muʿğam Dimašq at-tārīḫī*, 3 vols. (Damascus: Manšūrāt Wizārat aṯ-Ṯaqāfah, 1999), 2:322–23.

51. وَذَا عُلُومُ المَلَا عِنْدُه وَهو جَاهِلْ

52. وَذَا مُشَكَّلْ وَذَا مُهْمَلْ وَذَا عَاطِلْ

One is singing, one is leaving (spatially: stands outside; musically: sings out of tune, lacks the pitch), and the other is inside (spatially: coming in; musically: is in tune, has the proper pitch).[66]

One is claiming he is speaking the truth while plunging into nonsense.

One is claiming to have the knowledge of erudite men, while he was only primitive.

One is skittish, the other without attention, and that man is lazy.[67]

Further, Māmayh exemplifies the consequences of such habits from the perspective of women, who complain about their men hanging out in coffeehouses and thus being absent from their homes or not engaged in family affairs:

66 Māmayh uses this contrast (*dāḫil* and *ḫāriǧ*) in musical terms on other occasions. For the musical terminology, see Salah Eddin Maraqa: *Die traditionelle Kunstmusik in Syrien und Ägypten von 1500 bis 1800. Eine Untersuchung der musiktheoretischen und historisch-biographischen Quellen* (Tutzing: Hans Schneider, 2015), 278–80.

67 *ʿĀṭil* in the vernacular also means shifty/arrant. With *mušakkal*, *ʿāṭil*, and *muhmal* Māmayh alludes to the terminology of some of his constrained writing techniques (see chart above).

.62 تَقُولُ فِي بِيتْ قَهْوَهْ فَكَّرْتَك الهِيتْ

.63 وَلِحيْتكْ فِي حِكَايَاتِ الكَذِبْ هَزَّيتْ

She said: You have amused yourself in the coffeehouse,

and moved your beard (i.e., nodded your head) to tall tales.

.87 \266أ\ وَكُلَّمَا قُلْت له قُمْ يَا رَجُلْ جَامِـعْ [read: قُلْتَلُ]

.88 يَقُول قَصْدِي أصلّي الصُّبْحَ فِي الجَامِـعْ

Whenever I said to him: man, come on, go to the mosque! (unite!/ join/fuck me!),

he replied: Actually, I wanted to join the morning prayer in the mosque.[68]

Finally, the complaints and prayers of the narrating women are heard and the imperial decree on the closure of the coffee houses is issued. The closure, at least according to the poem, was carried out by the Qāḍī in Damascus, but as subsequent decrees prove, the closure did not last long:

.95 لَكِنْ أَنَا أَسْأَلْ بِمَنْ أَنْشَأَ السَّمَا وَالأَرضْ

.96 يقْرُضْ بيُوتِ القَهَاوِي فِي المَدِينَه قَرَضْ

.97 سَمَعْ دُعَاهَا مُهيْمِنْ ينْصِف المَظْلُومْ

68 Note the *ǧinās* with *ǧāmiʿ* and *al-ǧāmiʿ*.

98. وَأَصْبَحْ مُنَادِي عَلَى القَهْوَه مَعَهْ مَرْسُومْ

99. مِنْ ابْنِ عُثْمَان سُلْطَانْ العَرَبْ وَالرُّومْ

But I asked God who created the heavens and earth:

"May the coffee houses close down in the city," and they indeed did.

He heard her prayers and aided the wronged ones.

A proclaimer appeared to call out against coffee, carrying the decree astute

of the son of ʿUṯmān (i.e., Sulaymān), the Sultan of the Arabs and Rome.[69]

The theme of closing coffee houses continues in another *mawāliyā*. This may be about the same event, however, it remains somewhat ambiguous:[70]

---

69 *ar-Rūm*= for the Turks and people in the domains of the former Eastern Roman Empire.

70 From the second half of the 16th century, coffee houses in the province were closed repeatedly. See al-Arnāʾūṭ: *Min at-tārīḫ aṯ-ṯaqāfī li-l-qahwah,* 37–39. The first closure is dated by al-Arnāʾūṭ to 953/1545 at the intense instigation of Qāḍī Šayḫ Yūnus al-ʿĪtāwī, which was followed by another with an imperial decree (see, 39). Al-ʿArnāʾūṭ describes further decrees of Sultan Sulaymān for the closure for the years 973/1565, as well as in the following year (see, 40–41), though none for the year 966/1558, which Māmayh mentions in his poem. From the hitherto explored *muhimme defterleri* of the Ottoman Archives, Idris Bostan reports the following dates for closures: 966/1559 in Ḥoms, 972/1575 in Aleppo, Damascus, and al-Quds, 974/1577 in Cairo and Istanbul/Eyüp district, and 975/Istanbul; see Bostan: "Kahve", in: *TDVIA* (online).

[#807] وفيه أَيْضًا [مواليا]

1 ثَوْبُ الْحِدَادِ عَلَى الْقَهْوَةْ غَدَا مِدْرَارْ

وَالْبُنُّ قَلْبُهْ تَقَلَّا وَاحْتَرَقْ بِالنَّارْ

2 وَمِنْ سَمَا حَانِهَا قَدْ غَابَتِ الأَقْمَارْ

وَفِي الفَنَاجِينِ لَاحَ الْكَسْرُ بِالإِجْهَارْ

The mourning (lit.: robe) about the coffee became more and more abundant

as the heart of her bean has been roasted and burned in fire.

The moons (i.e., the cupbearers) had disappeared from the heaven of her place[71]

and the porcelain cups showed cracks openly.

When Nāṣir ad-Dīn al-Kišk (919–982/1513–1574), with whom Māmayh worked at the court, dared to compare the black coffee with the black stone of the Kaʿbah obviously to point to the magnetic pull of both, Māmayh rebuked and cursed him ironically using the voice of the coffee:[72]

[#1295] [بَحْرُ السَّرِيع]

71 *Ḥān*: tavern, coffeehouse or read *ḥāl*: her situation.

72 Note the antithesis (*al-aswad* and *bayyaḍa*) and the implied contrast between solid stone and liquid coffee.

1 قَدْ قَالَتِ القَهْوَةُ عَمَّنْ غَدَا — بِقُبْحِ تَشْبِيهٍ لَهَا تَعْتَدِي

2 لَا بَيَّضَ الرَّحْمَنُ وَجْهَ الَّذِي — شَبَّهَنِي بِالحَجَرِ الأَسْوَدِي

The coffee said about the one who came over with a despicable comparison and has thereby crossed the line.

May God the Beneficent not cheer him (lit. not whiten the face of the one) who compared me with the black stone!

Coffee is a particularly fruitful subject for poetic comparisons, which originate above all in wine poetry, as they share several associations, including: the tavern, conviviality, the dishes, the play of colors, the intoxication, the bubbles, the presentation of the drink, consumption traditions etc. Also, its functional elements as an irritant, of deliberately violating public morals are also employable in poetic speech. But it is also relatively easy to embed coffee thematically in a love poem or other genres. Based on the coffee poems, we can see very well how a current and indeed relatively new theme has found its way into poetry within classical imagery. It is integrated effortlessly into existing genres without being completely absorbed by them, as happened for a long period, for example, with water poetry.[73]

Arabic poetry of the pre-modern period is equally committed to tradition and innovation. Memoria, mimesis and the modern were chosen as anchor-points to show different scales of acts of embedding the past into the poet's present: through poetically organized patterns of remembrance,

---

73 Masarwa: "Wasser, Wein und Architektur. Kulissen des Genusses im *Ḥalbat al-Kumayt*", in: *The Racecourse of Literature: an-Nawāǧī and His Contemporaries*, edited by Alev Masarwa, and Hakan Özkan (Baden-Baden: Ergon 2020), 278–362.

explicit intertextual borrowings, and their emulation, or by connecting a new motif to classical patterns of imagery.

Modernist criticism, as directed against 'classical' poetry, based its arguments predominantly on the belief that the centuries-old conventions have led to a paralysed, shackled language, that inhibited free expression.[74] Thus, the entire impact of a political and socioeconomic ideology of liberation was imposed on the literary arts, which essentially have always been open. It was precisely literary tradition itself that required the poet to be innovative if he wanted to call himself a poet. And it was the same tradition that actualized itself anew through each newly crafted verse, and thus protected itself from being stifled. To invoke Shklovsky, "art [...] cannot afford routine" and "it was this deviation", insisted Shklovsky, this 'quality of divergence' that lay at the core of aesthetic perception."[75] Within such a system, the new and the innovative in pre-modern poetry may not always come with noisy ruptures and discontinuities,[76] but in a more moderate yet perceptible way in continuity with their conventions.

---

[74] For an ardent advocate of the renewal movements, see for example, Taha Hussein: "The Modern Renaissance of Arabic Literature [1955]", in: *World Literature Today* 63,2 (1989), 250. For a broader perspective, see Paul Starkey: *Modern Arabic Literature* (Edinburgh: Edinburgh University Press, 2006) and Salma Khadra Jayyusi: *Trends and Movements in Modern Arabic Poetry*, 2 vols. (Leiden: Brill, 1977). For a detailed discussion of the modernist movements and their positions on literary heritage, see Muhsin J. al-Musawi: *Arabic Poetry. Trajectories of Modernity and Tradition* (London: Routledge, 2006), esp. ch. 2–3.

[75] Viktor Erlich: *Russian Formalism*. Fourth edition (The Hague: Mounton, 1980), 252.

[76] As Adnan Haydar states: "What characterizes modernity in Arabic poetry is the rupture or the discontinuity which separates it from the conventions of classical Arabic verse." See idem: "What is Modern About Modern Arabic Poetry?" in: *Al-ʿArabiyya* 14 (1981), 51.

Accordingly, the question is not *if* Māmayh was innovative – as one would expect nothing else from a poet of his calibre – but *how*.[77]

It is perhaps one of the great fallacies of the 'modernists', that tradition and innovation were considered as necessarily excluding each other. I have tried to show how deeply Māmayh's poetry is anchored in the poetic tradition of his predecessors, while his own signature, his artistry and cunning versatility in style and form remain quite visible. The awareness of a rich legacy does not constitute the presence of the "burden of the past", as Jackson Bates states, but is a challenge to be faced, and there is not so much a reflection of any Bloomian "anxiety of influence", but a joy in communicating with the paragons of the past. Literary heritage thus serves as the broad operative playing field on which the innovative is performed, and it provides the foundation on which the innovation is recognized as such in the first place.

77 I hinted at some reasons *why* certain motifs or genres were preferred by Māmayh. However, it should become more apparent as further research on the topics is conducted, also by the correlating historical disciplines.

Appendix

MS Wetzstein II 243, Staatsbibliothek zu Berlin

#36 [fol. 13b]; #37 [fol. 13b–14a]; #63 [fol. 21b–22a]; #127 [fol. 39b]; #167 [fol. 53a–53b]; #168 [fol. 53b]; #228 [fol. 71a–72a]; #241 [fol. 76b]; #272 [fol. 86b]; #347 [fol. 129b–130a]; #382 [fol. 135b]; #384 [fol. 136a]; #385 [fol. 136a]; #432 [fol. 141b]; #433 [fol. 141b]; #434 [fol. 141b]; #455 [fol. 143b]; #475 [fol. 145b]; #476 [fol. 146a]; #492 [fol. 147b]; #493 [fol. 147b]; #494 [fol. 147b]; #496 [fol. 148a]; #512 [fol. 149a]; #513 [fol. 149a]; #520 [fol. 150a]; #526 [fol. 151a]; #553 [fol. 153a–153b]; #555 [fol. 153b]; #603 [fol. 158a]; #605 [fol. 158a]; #606 [fol. 158a]; #610 [fol. 158b]; #611 [fol. 158b]; #627 [fol. 160b]; #631 [fol. 161a]; #682 [fol. 166b]; #683 [fol. 166b]; #696 [fol. 167b–168a]; #704 [fol. 168b]; #705 [fol. 168b]; #718 [fol. 169b]; #746 [fol. 172a]; #777 [fol. 175a]; #782 [fol. 175b]; #804 [fol. 178a]; #807 [fol. 178b]; #808 [fol. 178b]; #839 [fol. 182a–184b]; #855 [fol. 186a]; #890 [fol. 189b]; #909 [fol. 191a]; #921 [fol. 192a]; #933 [fol. 193a]; #988 [fol. 218b–219a]; #991 [fol. 220a]; #993 [fol. 220b–221a]; #997 [fol. 222b–223a]; #998 [fol. 223a, 223b]; #1039 [fol. 277b–278b]; #1044 [fol. 284a–286a]; #1048 [fol. 292b–293b]; #1049 [fol. 293b–295a]; #1057 [fol. 301a–302b]; #1063 [fol. 303b]; #1065 [fol. 304b–305b]; #1068 [fol. 306a]; #1116 [fol. 321b]; #1123 [fol. 323a–324a]

MS Wetzstein II 163 Staatsbibliothek zu Berlin (ز)

MS Manchester 478, John Rylands Library Manchester (ط)

#1138 [(ز), fol. 91a–91b; (ط), 78b]; #1148 [(ط), fol. 107a]; #1149 [(ط), fol. 167b–168a]; #1150 [(ط), fol. 168a–168b]; #1152 [(ط), fol. 168b]; #1156 [(ز), fol. 267a; (ط), fol. 161a]; #1203 [(ز), fol. 275a]; #1219 [(ز), fol. 278a]; #1226 [(ز), fol. 279a]; #1227 [(ز), fol. 279a]; #1230 [(ز), fol. 279a]; #1273 [(ز), fol. 283a]; #1274 [(ز), fol. 283a]; #1295 [(ز), fol. 285b–286a]; #1319 [(ط), fol. 173b]; #1323 [(ط), fol. 173b]

Poem #228

وقال يذكر القرونَ الماضية [من الرمل]

1 لَيْسَ لِلنَّاسِ مِنَ الْمَوْتِ مَفَرْ ... وَلَكَمْ غَيَّبَ بَدْواً وَحَضَرْ

2 وَإِذَا فَكَّرَ فِيهِ عَاقِلٌ ... سَكَبَ العَبْرَةَ مِنْ هَوْلِ الْعِبَرْ

3 كَيْفَ فِي دَارِ الفَنَا يُرْجَى الْبَقَا ... إِنَّ هَذَا مِنْ خَيَالَاتِ الْفِكَرْ

4 فَازَ مَنْ قَدَّمَ أُخْرَاهُ عَلَى ... هَذِهِ الدُّنْيَا وَبِالْمَوْتِ اعْتَبَرْ

5 أَيْنَ يَا مَغْرُورُ قُلْ لِي آدَمٌ ... أَيْنَ إِدْرِيسُ وَنُوحٌ فِي الْبَشَرْ

6 أَيْنَ أَهْلُ الرَّسِّ وَالإِبْلِ الَّذِي ... عَبَدُوا مِنْ جَهْلِهِمْ حَتَّى الشَّجَرْ

7 أَيْنَ إِبْرَاهِيمُ أَعْنِي بِالَّذِي ... قَدْ بَنَى البَيْتَ المُعَلَّى وَالْحَجَرْ

8 أَيْنَ هُودٌ أَيْنَ قُلْ لِي صَالِحٌ ... مَنْ لَهُ نَاقَةُ شِرْبٍ مُحْتَضَرْ

9 أَيْنَ عَادٌ وَثَمُودٌ فِي الْمَلَا ... أَيْنَ مَنْ أَطْغَوْا تَعَاطَى فَعَقَرْ

10 أَيْنَ شَدَّادُ الَّذِي فَخْرًا بَنَى ... جَنَّةً فِي أَرْضِهَا دُرُّ الدُّرَرْ

11 أَيْنَ فِرْعَوْنُ الَّذِي مِنْ جَهْلِهِ ... قَالَ إِنِّي رَبُّكُمْ لَمَّا كَفَرْ

12 أَيْنَ مُوسَى مَنْ رَأَى نَاراً عَلَى ... جَبَلِ الطُّورِ بِلَيْلٍ اِعْتَكَرْ

13 فَدَنَا مُقْتَبِسًا مِنْ نُورِهَا ... سَمِعَ القَوْلَ أَنَا اللهُ فَخَرْ

14 \71ب\ أَيْنَ هَامَانُ الَّذِي مِنْ كُفْرِهِ ... قَدْ بَنَى صَرْحًا مُعَلًّا فَانْدَثَرْ

15 أَيْنَ قَارُونُ الَّذِي زِينَتُهُ　　خَلَّفَتْهُ تَحْتَ خَسْفٍ لَا مَقَرْ

16 أَيْنَ دَاوُدُ الَّذِي فِتْنَتُهُ　　قَتَلَتْ نَفْساً وَمَوْلَاهُ غَفَرْ

17 أَيْنَ هُوَ مُلْكُ سُلَيْمَانَ الَّذِي　　لَمْ يَنَلْهُ غَيْرُهُ طُولَ الدَّهَرْ

18 أَيْنَ لُقْمَانُ الَّذِي حِكْمَتُهُ　　نَفْعُهَا لِلآنَ مِنْ كُلِّ ضَرَرْ

[أَيْنَ ذو القرنين مَن طافَ في الـ　　ـشرقِ والغربِ وبالخضر اِنْتَصَرْ]

19 أَيْنَ رُوحُ اللهِ عِيسَى وَالَّذِي　　قَدْ أَقَامَ الْمَيْتَ مِنْ طِينِ الْحَجَرْ

20 أَيْنَ أَفْلَاطُونُ رَاسُ الْحُكَمَا　　وَأَرِسْطُو مَنْ بِفَضْلٍ اشْتُهِرْ

21 أَيْنَ سَاسَانٌ وَمَنْ قَدْ مَلَكُوا　　أَيْنَ كِسْرَى مَنْ لِأَعْدَاهُ كَسَرْ

22 أَيْنَ قُلْ لِي قَيْصَرُ الرُّومِ الَّذِي　　مَلَكَ الأَرْضَ وَبِالْمُلْكِ افْتَخَرْ

23 أَيْنَ طَهَ الْمُصْطَفَى وَالْمُجْتَبَى　　خَاتَمُ الرُّسْلِ وَبِالْحَقِّ أَمَرْ

24 زُبْدَةُ الْكَوْنِ الَّذِي لَوْلَاهُ مَا　　خَلَقَ الرَّحْمَنُ شَمْساً وَقَمَرْ

25 أَيْنَ صِدِّيقٌ تَسَامَى صِدْقُهُ　　أَيْنَ فَارُوقُ الْهُدَى أَعْنِي عُمَرْ

26 أَيْنَ ذُو النُّورَيْنِ عُثْمَانُ العُلَا　　وَعَلِيُّ الْمُرْتَضَى سَامِي الْفَخَرْ

27 أَيْنَ نُورُ الْعَيْنِ أَعْنِي حَسَناً　　مَنْ ثَوَى بِالسُّمِّ فِي قَاعِ الْحُفَرْ

28 أَيْنَ مَنْ فِي كَرْبَلَا قَاسَى الْبَلَا　　وَعَلَى بَلْوَاهُ بِاللهِ صَبَرْ

29 أَيْنَ مَرْوَانُ الَّذِي فِتْنَتُهُ　　أَثَّرَ مِن حُمْقِهِ أَرْدَى الأَثَرْ

30	أَيْنَ مَنْ قَدْ مَلَكَ الشَّامَ مِنَ الْ	أُمَوِيِّينَ إِلَى أَقْصَى التَّتَرْ
31	\72\أَيْنَ سَادَاتٌ كِرَامٌ خَلَفُوا	مِنْ بَنِي العَبَّاسِ هَلْ عَنْهُمْ خَبَرْ
32	أَيْنَ قُلْ لِي آلُ حَمْدَانَ الَّذِي	مِنْهُمُ سَيْفٌ وَكَمْ فَضْلٍ شُهِرْ
33	أَيْنَ نُورُ الدِّينِ وَالأَكْرَادُ مَنْ	ذِكْرُهُمْ بِالجُودِ فِي الْكَوْنِ ظَهَرْ
34	أَيْنَ تُرْكٌ تُرْكُمَانٌ جَرْكَسٌ	تَرَكُوا المُلْكَ لِغَيْرٍ بِالْغِيَرْ
35	أَيْنَ غُورِيهَا الَّذِي غَوَّرَهُ [غَوْرِيها]	حَاكِمُ الْكَوْنِ سَلِيمُ الْمُعْتَبَرْ
36	أَيْنَ سُلْطَانُ سُلَيْمَانُ الَّذِي	قَدْ أَسَرَّ الدِّينَ وَالْكُفْرَ أَسَرْ
37	أَيْنَ سُلْطَانُ سَلِيمٌ أَيْنَ الَّذِي	كَانَ ثَانٍ فَاعْتَبِرْ ~~[يَا]~~ أَهْلَ النَّظَرْ
38	فَاعْتَبِرْ بِالمَوْتِ يَا هَذَا فَكَمْ	عَاقِلٍ دُنْيَاهُ غَرَّتْ بِالغُرَرْ
39	وَاسْأَلِ اللهَ تَعَالَى رَحْمَةً	بِخِتَامِ الخَيْرِ فِي مَوْتٍ حَضَرْ
40	وَاطْلُبِ الْعَفْوَ مِنَ الْمَوْلَى وَقُلْ	رَبِّ لُطْفًا فِي قَضَاءٍ وَقَدَرْ

Translation [#228]

[…]

8. And where is Hūd? And tell me where is Ṣāliḥ / whose she-camel drinking was attended? [Q 54:27–28, Q 7:73, Q 26: 155, Q 11:64]

9. And where is ʿĀd and Ṯamūd / among the eminent ones? / And where are those, who have transgressed (the bounds of

law) / when they in their rebellious pride hamstrung the she-camel? [Q 11:112; Q 91:11, Q 54:29]

10. And where is Šaddād, who out of pride built a paradise, where there were the most precious pearls on its ground? [~Q 89:6–8]

11. Where is Pharaoh, who out of ignorance claimed, "I am your God!" when he was infidel? [Q 28:38]

12. Where is Moses, who saw a fire in a turbid night at the mountain aṭ-Ṭūr? [Q 28:28–29; 19:52]

13. and who, as he approached it to take a brand of it heard (God) saying: "I am God!" and whereupon he fell down? [Q 29:29; Q 52; Q 27:7; Q 20:10; Q 7:143]

14. Where is Hāmān, who from his disbelief built a lofty tower, which collapsed? [Q 28:38; Q 40:36]

15. Where is Qārūn, whose adornment caused him to be swallowed into a deep place in the ground, that is bottomless (altern.: left him behind under vileness which has no ground)? [Q 28:79]

16. And where is David, whose wrongdoing has caused the loss of life? and God forgave him (after he repented)? [Q 38:17–25]

17. Where is the kingdom of Solomon, who possessed what no one ever possessed?

18. Where is Luqmān, whose wisdom still saves us from harm? [Q 31]

[19. Where is Ḏū l-Qarnayn, who travelled from East to West and, who with al-Ḫiḍr was triumphant?][78] [Q 18:83, 86, 94; ~ al-Ḫiḍr Q 18:65]

19. Where is Jesus the spirit of God, who (made alive) brought to life, raised from the "dead" matter of stone (or bird of stone) altern.; who put to life the bird of stone? [Q 5:110; Q 3:49]

20. Where is Plato, the head of the philosophers and Aristotle, thus became famous by his excellence?

21. Where is Sāsān and where are those, who possessed the dominions, where Kisrā was defeated by his enemies?

22. Where is the king (qayṣar, Caesar) of Rome, who reigned the world and boasted about his possessions?[79]

23. Where is Ṭāhā l-Muṣṭafā, the chosen one, / the seal of messengers, who commanded with divine truth (of the Almighty),

24. the best of the universe? If it were not for him, God would not have created the sun and the moon.

25. Where is Ṣiddīq? May he be elevated by his truthfulness! And where is Fārūq, the arbiter of the right guidance, I mean ʿUmar?

26. Where is ʿUṯmān the exalted possessor of the two lights and ʿAlī (the Exalted), with whom God is pleased, may his glory be augmented!

---

78 This verse is missing in some mss.

79 Māmayh most probably meant the Byzantine emperor, otherwise there would be a chronological inconsistency if Māmayh meant Caesar.

27. Where is the light of the eye, I mean Ḥasan, who rests poisoned on the ground of a pit (of ambush)?

28. Where is he, who had to endure severest suffering, who endured his torment – by God!– with forbearance?

29. Where is Marwān, whose wrongdoing … caused by his stupidity spoiled the relics (or traces of tradition)?

30. Where are those, who ruled Syria from the House of Umayyah right up to the Tatars?

31. Where are those honored/dignified people, who followed the House of ʿAbbās, is there any trace of them?

32. And where is, tell me, the House of Ḥamdān, of whom Sayf and so many excellencies are famous?

33. Where is Nūr ad-Dīn and the Kurds, who are remembered as the benevolent /generous?

34. Where are the Turkoman, Turks, Circassians, who left their dominions to one another in rivalry?

35. Where is their Ġawrī, who has been dashed to the ground by Selīm (i.e., Selim I), the respected ruler of the world?

36. Where is Sulṭān Sulaymān, who gladdened the belief, and put the unbelief in chains?[80]

37. Where is Sulṭān Selīm, where is the one, who was the second (i.e., Selīm II)? You eminent people, just consider!

---

[80] *asara*= to bind, to captivate, here in a positive phrasing.

38. Just consider death, oh you. The lives of how many sane people were blinded by delusion.

39. I ask God in his mercy for a blessed ending, for death is all-present.

40. And you, seek the Lord for forgiveness and say be merciful in (your) divine will and decree (i.e., in fate and destiny).

Bibliography

Dīwān-Manuscripts

MS Alexandria 2079 (ق)

MS Bengal Asiatic Society 686 (ع)

MS Berlin Staatsbibliothek Wetzstein II 163 (ز)

MS Manchester 478, John Rylands Library Manchester (ط)

MS Patna 1786 (د)

MS Princeton University Library, HSVM Islamic Manuscripts, Third Series no. 85 (ر)

MS Riad 811; *Burdah-Taḫmīs* (خ)

MS Wetzstein II 163 Staatsbibliothek zu Berlin (ز)

MS Wetzstein II 243, Staatsbibliothek zu Berlin

Sources and Studies

ʿAbd al-ʿAzīz, ʿId Fatḥī: *Al-Ittiğahāt al-adab al-ʿarabī fī l-qarn al-ḥādī ʿašar al-hiğrī*. PhD diss., ʿAyn Šams University: Kulliyat al-Ādāb, Cairo, 1426-27/2005-6.

Altunğī, Muḥammad: *Al-Ittiğāhāt aš-šiʿriyyah fī bilād aš-Šām fī l-ʿaṣr al-ʿUṯmānī: dirāsah*. Damascus: Ittiḥād al-Kuttāb al-ʿArab, 1993.

Amīn, Bakrī Šayḫ: *Muṭālaʿāt fī š-šiʿr al-Mamlūkī wa-l-ʿUṯmānī*. Cairo: Dār aš-Šurūq, 1972.

ʿAnūtī, Usāmah: *al-Ḥarakah al-adabiyyah fī bilād aš-Šām ḫilāl al-qarn aṯ-ṯamin ʿašar*. Beirut: Lebanese University Press, 1970.

al-Arnāʾūṭ, Muḥammad M.: *Min at-tārīḫ aṯ-ṯaqāfī li-l-qahwah wa-l-maqāhī*. Beirut: Ǧadāwil, 2012.

al-ʿAydarūs: *an-Nūr as-sāfir ʿan aḫbār al-qarn al-ʿāšir*, edited by Aḥmad Ḥālū, Maḥmūd al-Arnāʾūṭ, and Akram Albūšī. Beirut: Dār Ṣādir, 2001.

al-Bakr, Maḥmūd Mufliḥ: *al-Qahwah al-ʿarabiyyah fī l-mawrūṯ wa-l-adab aš-šaʿbī*. Beirut: Bīsān li-n-Našr wa-t-Tawzīʿ wa-l-Iʿlām, 1995.

Beard, Michael: "Review of "Essays in Arabic Literary Biography 1350–1850." In: *Journal of the American Oriental Society* 132 (2012), pp. 486–488.

Berndt, Frauke: "Poetische Topik." In: *Handbuch Literarische Rhetorik*, edited by Rüdiger Zymner. Berlin/Boston: de Gruyter, 2015, pp. 433–460.

Bīrahǧaklī, Zaynab: *al-Ḥarakah aš-šiʿriyyah fī Ḥalab: fī l-qarn al-ḥādī ʿašar al-hiǧrī*. ʿAmmān: Dār aḍ-Ḍiyāʾ, 1444/2001.

Borysowska, Agnieszka and Milewska-Waźbińska, Barbara: "Introductionary Note." In: *Poesis Artificiosa. Between Theory and Practice*, ed. eadem. Frankfurt, a. M.: Peter Lang Acad. Research, 2013, pp. 7–8.

Bostan, Idris: "Kahve." In: TDVİA= Türkiye Diyanet Vakfı İslâm Ansiklopedisi İslâm Ansiklopedisi https://islamansiklopedisi.org.tr/kahve (25.07.2021).

Bosworth, Clifford Edmund: "A Janissary poet of sixteenth-century Damascus." In: *Essays in honor of Bernard Lewis. The Islamic world, classical and medieval, Ottoman and modern*, eds C. E. Bosworth et al. Princeton: Darwin Press, 1989, pp. 451–66.

Brockelmann, Carl: [*GAL*] *Geschichte der arabischen Litteratur,* 2 vols. [2]Leiden: Brill, 1943–1949.

Brockelmann, Carl: [*GALS*] *Geschichte der arabischen Litteratur. Supplementbände I-III.* Leiden: Brill, 1937–1942.

Brogan, Terry V.F.: "Rhetoric and Poetry." In: *The New Princeton Encyclopedia of Poetry and Poetics. Princeton*, edited by Alex Preminger, T.V.F. Brogan et al. Princeton, N.J.: Princeton University Press, 1993, pp. 1045–52.

Brookes, Douglas cf. Gelibolulu.

Cachia, Pierre: *The arch rhetorician or the schemer's skimmer: A handbook of late Arabic badīʿ drawn from ʿAbd al-Ghanī an-Nābulsī's* Nafaḥāt al-azhār ʿalā nasamāt al-asḥār, *summarized and systematized*. Wiesbaden: Harrassowitz, 1998.

Cachia, Pierre: "The Egyptian Mawwāl." In: *Journal of Arabic Literature* 8 (1977), pp. 77–103.

Ceviz, Nurettin: "Kahvenin İslâm Dünyasına Girişi ve Arap Edebiyatında Ele Alınışı." in: *EKEV Akademi Dergisi* 18 (2004), pp. 343–56.

Erlich, Viktor: *Russian Formalism*. The Hague: Mounton, [4]1980.

Fidan, İbrahim: *Osmanlı Dönemi Arap Şairlerinden İbnu'n Nakib el-Huseyni*. Ankara: Gece Kitaplığı, 2016.

Gelibolulu Mustafa Âli: *The Ottoman Gentlemen of the sixteenth Century, Mustafa ʿAli's 'Tables of Delicacies Concerning the Rules of Social Gatherings'* [Mevāʾidüʾn-nefāʾis fī ḳavāʿidiʾl-mecālis]. Translated by Douglas Brookes. Cambridge [Mass.]: Harvard University, 2003.

Güneş, Ahmet Halil: *Das Kitāb ar-rauḍ al-ʿāṭir des Ibn-Aiyūb. Damaszener Biographien des 10./16. Jahrhunderts*. Berlin: Schwarz-Verlag, 1971.

Gunning, Tom: "Re-Newing Old Technologies: Astonishment, Second Nature, and the Un-canny in Technology from the Previous Turn-of-the-Century." In: *Rethinking Media Change: The Aesthetics of Transition*, edited by David Thorburn, and Henry Jenkins. Cambridge [Mass.]: MIT Press, 2003, pp. 39–60.

al-Ġuzūlī, ʿAlāʾ ad-Dīn ʿAlī b. ʿAbdallāh: *Maṭālīʿ l-budūr fī manāzil as-surūr*, edited by Saʿīd Maḥmūd at-Tiǧānī. Vol. 1, 2 vols. Beirut: Dār al-Kutub al-ʿIlmiyyah, 1438/2017.

al-Ḫafāǧī, Šihāb ad-Dīn: *Ḫabāyā z-zawāyā fī mā fī r-riǧāl min al-baqāyā*, eds. Muḥammad Masʿūd Arkīn [Ergin] et al. Damascus, Maṭbūʿāt Maǧmaʿ al-Luġah al-ʿArabiyyah bi-Dimašq, 1436/2010.

Hattox, Ralf S.: *Coffee and Coffeehouses. The Origins of a Social Beverage in Medieval Near East*. Seattle/London: University of Washington Press, [3]1996.

Haydar, Adnan: "What is Modern About Modern Arabic Poetry?" In: *Al-ʿArabiyya* 14 (1981), pp. 51–8.

Hoenerbach, Wilhelm: "Zwei Studien zur spanisch-arabischen Literatur." In: *ZDMG* 141 (1991), pp. 253–80.

Hussein, Taha: "The Modern Renaissance of Arabic Literature [1955]." In: *World Literature Today* 63,2 (1989), pp. 249–56.

Ibn Abī l-Iṣbaʿ al-Miṣrī: *Taḥrīr at-taḥbīr fī ṣināʿat aš-šiʿr wa-n-naṯr wa-bayān iʿǧāz l-Qurʾān*, ed. Ḥifnī Muḥammad Šaraf. Cairo: al-Maǧlis al-Aʿlā li-š-Šuʾūn al-Islāmiyyah, Laǧnat Iḥyā at-Turāṯ al-Islāmī, [1963].

Ibn Ayyūb, Šaraf ad-Dīn: *Kitab ar-rawḍ al-ʿāṭir*, edited by Mašhūr al-Ḥabbāzī, 2 vols. Beirut: Dār al-Kutub al-ʿIlmiyyah, 1441/2020.

Ibn Ayyūb, Šaraf ad-Dīn: *at-Taḏkirah [al-Ayyūbiyyah]*, MS aẓ-Ẓāhiriyyah 7814, Damascus.

Ibn Ḥiǧǧah: *Ḫizānat al-adab wa-ġāyat al-arab*, edited by Kawkab Diyāb. Vol. 4, 5 vols. Beirut: Dār Ṣādir, 2005.

Ibn Mulayk al-Ḥamawī: *Dīwān al-nafaḥāt al-adabiyyah min al-zahrāt al-Ḥamawiyyah*, edited by Isrāʾ Aḥmad Fawzī al-Hayb. Damascus: Manšūrāt al-Hayʾah al-ʿĀmmah as-Sūriyah li-l-Kutub, 2010.

Ibn Nubātah: *Dīwān Ibn Nubātah al-Miṣrī*, edited by Muḥammad al-Qalqīlī. Cairo/Miṣr: Maṭbaʿat at-Tamaddun, 1323/1905.

Ibn ar-Rāʿī: *al-Barq al-mutaʾalliq fī maḥāsīn Ǧilliq*, ed. Muḥammad al-Gādir. Damascus: Maṭbuʿāt Maǧmaʿ al-Luġah al-ʿArabiyyah bi-Dimašq, 1429/2008.

Jacob, Georg: *Ein ägyptischer Jahrmarkt im 13. Jahrhundert*. München: Verlag der Königlich Bayerischen Akademie der Wissenschaften, 1910.

Jayyusi, Salma Khadra. *Trends and Movements in Modern Arabic Poetry*, 2 vols., Leiden: Brill, 1977.

Karababa, Eminegül, and Ger, Güliz: "Early Modern Ottoman Coffeehouse Culture and the Formation of the Consumer Subject." In: *Journal of Consumer Research* 37 (2011), pp. 737–60.

Küçüksarı, Mücahit: *Osmanlı Dönemi Arap Şairlerinden İbrahim Es-Sefercelani ve Şiirleri*. Konya: Çizgi Kitabevi, 2017.

Lachmann, Renate: "Cultural Memory and the Role of Literature." In: *European Review* 12 (2004), pp. 165–78.

Lachmann, Renate: "Kalligraphie, Arabeske, Phantasma. Zur Semantik der Schrift in Prosatexten des 19. Jahrhunderts." In: *Poetica* 29 (1997), pp. 455-98.

Lachmann, Renate: "Mnemonic and Intertextual Aspects of Literature." In *Cultural Memory Studies. An International and Interdisciplinary Handbook*, edited by Astrid Erll, and Ansgar Nünning. Berlin/New York: de Gruyter 2008, pp. 301–10.

Larkin, Margret: "The Dust of the Master. A Mamlūk-Era 'Zajal' by Khalaf al-Ghubārī." In: *Quaderni di Studi Arabi, N.S.* 2 (2007), pp. 11–29.

Lowry, Joseph E. and Stewart Devin J.: "Introduction." In: *Essays in Arabic Literary Biography 1350–1850*, ed. by Joseph E. Lowry and Devin J. Stewart. Wiesbaden: Harrassowitz, 2009, pp. 1–12.

Maraqa, Salah Eddin: *Die traditionelle Kunstmusik in Syrien und Ägypten von 1500 bis 1800. Eine Untersuchung der musiktheoretischen und historisch-biographischen Quellen*. Tutzing: Hans Schneider, 2015.

Masarwa, Alev: "Ibn Mulayk." In: *Encyclopaedia of Islam Three* (2022, online).

Masarwa, Alev: "Māmayh im Prophetenmantel: Ornat, Saum und Zipfel der *Burdah* im *Taḫmīs*." In: *Emerging Forms of Piety Centering on Muḥammad as Reflected in Arabic Literature*, ed. Ines Weinrich. Baden-Baden: Ergon, upcoming 2022.

Masarwa, Alev: "Māmayh Muḥammad b. Aḥmad b. ʿAbdallāh ar-Rūmī." In: *Encyclopaedia of Islam Three* (upcoming).

Masarwa, Alev: "Performing the Occasion: The Chronograms of Māmayya ar-Rūmī." In: *The Mamluk-Ottoman Transition: Continuity and Change in Egypt and Bilād al-Shām in the Sixteenth Century*, edited by Stephan Conermann, and Gül Şen. Göttingen: Vandenhoeck & Ruprecht Verlage, 2017, pp. 177-206.

Masarwa, Alev: "Poetisch wider Willen: Der Koran im Vers Māmayhs. Über poetische Verfahren der Doppel- bzw. Mehrfachcodierung und des Code-Switching in *iqtibās*-Epigrammen." In: *Doing Justice to a Wronged Literature: Essays in Honour of Professor Thomas Bauer on his Sixtieth Birthday*, edited by Nefeli Papoutsakis and Hakan Özkan. Leiden: Brill, upcoming 2022 (*Islamic History and Civilization: Studies and Texts*).

Masarwa, Alev: "Wasser, Wein und Architektur. Kulissen des Genusses im Ḥalbat al-Kumayt." In: *The Racecourse of Literature: an-Nawāǧī and His Contemporaries*, edited by Alev Masarwa, and Hakan Özkan. Baden-Baden: Ergon 2020, pp. 278–362.

al-Musawi, Muhsin Jasim: *Arabic Poetry. Trajectories of Modernity and Tradition*. London: Routledge, 2006.

Neuber, Wolfgang: "memoria." In: *Reallexikon der deutschen Literaturwissenschaft*, edited by Georg Braungart et al. Berlin/New York 2007, pp. 562–66.

Özkan, Hakan: *Geschichte des östlichen zağal – dialektale arabische Strophendichtung aus dem Osten der arabischen Welt von ihren Anfängen bis zum Ende der Mamlukenzeit*. Baden-Baden: Ergon-Verlag, 2020.

Öztürk, Zehra: "Eğitim Tarihimizde Okuma Toplantarının Yeri ve Okunan Kitaplar." In: *Değerler Eğitimi Dergisi* 1 (2003), pp. 131–155.

Péri, Benedek. "A Janissary's Son Turned Druggist and His Highly Successful Designer Drug in 16th–17th Century." In: *Osmanlı İstanbulu IV: Uluslararası Osmanlı İstanbulu Sempozyumu bildirileri, 20-22 Mayıs, İstanbul 29 Mayıs Üniversitesi*, edited by Feridun

M. Emecen, Ali Akyıldız, and Emrah Safa Gürkan. İstanbul: 29 Mayıs Üniversitesi Yayınları, 2016, pp. 643–54.

[al-Quraysī] Ḥammūd, Riḍā Muḥsin: *al-Funūn aš-šiʿriyya ġayr al-muʿraba: al-mawāliyā*. Baghdad: al-Maktabah al-Fūlklūriyyah, 1976.

Sajdi, Dana: "Decline, Its Discontents and Ottoman Cultural History: By Way of Introduction." In: *Ottoman Tulips, Ottoman Coffee: Leisure and Lifestyle in the Eighteenth Century*, edited by eadem. London: I.B. Tauris, 2014, pp. 1–40.

Samancı, Yusuf Sami: *Osmanlı dönemi Arap Şairlerinden Mencek Paşa ve Şiirleri*. Konya: Çizgi Kitabevi, 2017.

Sezen, Lütfi: *Halk Edebiyatında Hamzanâmeler*. Ankara: Kültür Bakanlığı Yayınları, 1991.

Sing, Manfred: "The Decline of Islam and the Rise of Inḥiṭāṭ: The Discrete Charm of Language Games about Decadence in the 19th and 20th Centuries." In: *Inḥiṭāṭ – The Decline Paradigm: Its Influence and Persistence in the Writing of Arab Cultural History*, edited by Syrinx von Hees. Würzburg: Ergon-Verlag, 2017, pp. 1–70.

aš-Šihābī, Qutaybah: *Muʿǧam Dimašq at-tārīḫī*. Vol. 2, 3 vols. Damascus: Manšūrāt Wizārat aṯ-Ṯaqāfah, 1999.

aš-Širwānī, Aḥmad ibn Muḥammad al-Anṣārī al-Yamanī: *Kitāb nafḥat al-Yaman fī mā yazūlu bi-ḏikrihi aš-šaǧan*. Miṣr: al-Maṭbaʿah al-ʿĀmirah aš-Šarqīyah, 1305 [1888].

Sīrat ʿAntarah b. Šaddād, edition Turāṯ. Vol. 3, 8 vols. [repr. of *Sīrat fāris fursān al-Ḥiǧāz Abī l-Fawāris ʿAntarah b. Šaddād: wa-hiya s-sīrah al-fāʾiqah al-ḥiǧāziyyah al-muštamilah ʿalā l-aḫbār al-aǧībah wa-l-anbāʾ al-ǧaliyyah*. 8 vols. (Beirut: al-Maktabah al-ʿIlmiyyah al-Ḥadīṯah, 1399/1979)] Beirut: Dār al-Kutub al-ʿIlmiyyah, 1980.

Starkey, Paul: *Modern Arabic Literature*. Edinburgh: Edinburgh University Press, 2006.

Trumpp, Ernst: "Der Bedingungssatz im Arabischen." In: *Sitzungsberichte der Philosophisch-philologischen und historischen Classe der Königlichen bayerischen Akademie der Wissenschaften zu München. Vol. 2, 2 vols.* München: Akademische Buchdruckerei von F. Straub, 1881, pp. 337–448.

Uluskan, Murat: "İstanbul'da Bir Afyonlu Macun İşletmesi: Berş-i Rahîkî Macunhanesi (1783–1831)." In: *Türk Kültürü İncelemeleri Dergisi* 29 (2013), pp. 77–106.

Van den Oever, Annie: "Ostranenie, 'The Montage of Attractions' and Early Cinema's 'Properly Irreducible Alien Quality'." In: *Ostrannenie. On "Strangeness" and the Moving Image. The History, Reception, and Relevance of a Conceptnull*, edited by eadem. Amsterdam: Amsterdam University Press, 2010, pp. 33–58.

Weil, Gustav: *Das Leben Muḥammed's nach Moḥammed Ibn Ishāk bearbeitet von Abd el-Malik Ibn Hishām*. Vol. 1, 2 vols. Stuttgart: Verlag der J. B. Metzler'schen Buchhandlung, 1864.

Zymner, Rüdiger: "Rhetorik, Literatur und Literaturwissenschaft." In: *Handbuch Literarische Rhetorik*, edited by Rüdiger Zymner. Berlin/Boston: de Gruyter, 2015, pp. 1–20.

FSC
www.fsc.org
MIX
Papier | Fördert
gute Waldnutzung
FSC® C083411

Zeitfracht Medien GmbH
Ferdinand-Jühlke-Straße 7
99095 Erfurt, Deutschland
produktsicherheit@kolibri360.de